A2 Geography
UNIT 4

AQA

Specification B

Module 4: Global Change

Geoff Farmer, David Redfern & Malcolm Skinner

Philip Allan Updates
Market Place
Deddington
Oxfordshire
OX15 0SE

tel: 01869 338652
fax: 01869 337590
e-mail: sales@philipallan.co.uk
www.philipallan.co.uk

This Guide has been written specifically to support students preparing for the
AQA Specification B A2 Geography Unit 4 examination. The content has been
neither approved nor endorsed by AQA and remains the sole responsibility of
the authors.

Printed by Information Press, Eynsham, Oxford

Contents

Introduction

■ ■ ■

Content Guidance

■ ■ ■

Questions and Answers

Introduction

About this guide

Students following the AQA Specification B A2 Geography course have to study **Module 4: Global Change**. They will be seeking to understand:

- the key ideas of the content of the module
- the nature of the assessment material by the consideration of sample structured questions
- the requirements to answer exam questions successfully

This guide provides opportunities to satisfy each of the above requirements.

This **Introduction** begins with advice on learning and revision techniques. It then provides an explanation of some of the key command words used in examination papers, together with guidance on how to answer questions requiring essays.

The **Content Guidance** section clarifies many aspects of the content of Module 4 so that the reader is made aware of the material that has to be learnt.

The **Question and Answer** section includes sample questions in the style of the unit test, together with a range of student responses. Each answer is followed by a detailed examiner's response. It is suggested that you read through the relevant topic area in the Content Guidance section before attempting a question from the Question and Answer section, and only read the specimen answers after you have tackled the question yourself.

Techniques for learning and revision

The aim of this section is to suggest some ways in which you can revise for the Unit 4 test. They cannot all work for you, so only choose the technique(s) that work(s) best for you. Whichever technique you choose, make sure you use it regularly.

Mind mapping

This is useful when trying to learn new information, or when trying to pull together material from a range of different areas. For example, look at the following mind map, which relates to international migration. Start with the term being considered in the centre of a piece of paper and ring it. Then consider the major subdivisions and place these around the edge of the ring, like branches. Then add further points that elaborate upon the initial term, with further subdivisions if necessary.

Each mind map is very personal to you, but it should enable you to remember the key points in a topic, and allow you to concentrate on them more quickly.

Pictorial notes

Some people have the ability to remember facts according to where they are located on a page of notes — they can be said to have a 'photographic memory'. Others exhibit a variation of this by remembering colours, and what facts are contained within different coloured areas of their notes.

Another aspect of this form of revision is to convert written notes into a sketch or picture, and to use this as a revision tool.

Fact cards

Here you write your own summary of the key points of a particular topic onto blank cards. You could transfer the contents of one A4 sheet of notes onto one card. The card(s) can be carried around with you to read during moments when you would otherwise be doing little, such as travelling to school or sitting in a common room. Maintain your cards in a logical order using a treasury tag.

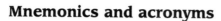

Mnemonics and acronyms

These are 'pegs' upon which you can hang specific memories. You can use either letters or words to construct a mnemonic. Mnemonics where the initial letters make up a word are called acronyms. As with mind maps, the use of these can be, and possibly should be, personal to you.

Flow diagrams

A flow diagram records inputs and outputs, and shows movement or links between places by means of boxes connected by simple directional arrows. You could try this approach to summarise the impacts of transnational corporations (TNCs).

Skeleton lists

This is perhaps the most basic way to assemble ideas in a logical order before completing the task of writing an answer. For example, when considering factors affecting soils, the following may apply:

- soil water
- soil air
- mineral matter
- time
- relief
- particle size
- weather and climate
- organic matter
- human activity

This list provides a skeleton around which a discussion of the factors affecting soil could be constructed.

The unit test

Command words

One of the pitfalls facing candidates is difficulty in interpreting the demands of the questions. Thorough revision is essential, but candidates also require an awareness of what is expected from them in the examination. Too often, candidates attempt to answer the question they think is there rather than the one that is actually set. Answering an examination question is challenging enough, without the extra self-imposed handicap of having misread the question.

Correct interpretation of the **command words** is therefore very important. In an A-level geography examination paper, a variety of command words are used. Some demand more of the candidate than others. They might require a relatively simple task to be performed or call for greater intellectual thought and synthesis. The major command words used in the unit test are described below.

Explain.../suggest reasons for/why.../how might...

These ask for a statement as to why something occurs. They test your ability to know or to understand why or how something happens. Question setters have tended to move away from using 'explain' and have moved more towards the command 'suggest reasons for/why'. The reason for this is that there are varying ways in which geographical changes and issues can be explained.

Give an explanatory account of.../give a reasoned account of...

These ask for a combination of the demands of a 'describe' question, and a 'suggest reasons why' question. The question setters have recognised that the logical way to present an answer is to provide a description of a feature, together with an explanation for it. Such questions tend to carry a large number of marks, and you are expected to write a relatively long piece of prose.

Using an annotated diagram...

Here you *must* draw a diagram. Annotations are labels that provide some additional description and/or explanation of the main features of the diagram.

Analyse...

This requires you to break down the content of a topic into its constituent parts, and to give an in-depth account. Again, such questions tend to carry a large number of marks, and you are expected to write a relatively long piece of prose.

Discuss...

This is one of the most common higher-level command words, and is used most often in questions that carry a large number of marks. You are expected to build up an argument about an issue, that is, to present more than one side to it. You should present arguments for and against, making good use of evidence and examples, and express an opinion about the merits of each side.

Developing essay skills

Developing essay-writing skills is not easy, but it is a real opportunity for you to impress, and to score at a higher level than your peers. All essays should have a beginning (the introduction), a middle (the argument) and an end (the conclusion).

The introduction

This does not have to be too long — a few sentence(s) should suffice. You could define some of the terms stated in the question, or you could set the scene for the argument to follow. Where the essay requires a particular idea, concept or viewpoint to be developed, then an initial statement of this could be given. Finally, if possible, be interesting — grab the reader!

The argument

This must consist of a series of paragraphs, which may present different sides of an argument. In principle, each paragraph should develop one point only, and should follow logically on from the previous one. Avoid paragraphs that list facts without any meaningful link back to the question. Such answers leave the interpretation too much in the hands of the reader/examiner, and so are not to be encouraged. Finally, in geographical essays, it is important to make good use of examples, i.e. real places (which could be local to you).

Conclusion

This should reiterate the introduction but this time supported by the evidence, arguments and facts given in the bulk of the response. A set of summative statements which refer clearly to the question should be provided. In the case of the command word 'discuss', the conclusion should point out those points in the original question that are valid, and those where there is debate or disagreement.

How are questions marked?

Examination questions in Unit 4 are marked according to fixed criteria. These criteria are based on your:

- **knowledge (K)** — of concepts, case studies and terminology
- **understanding (U)** — of processes, theories, ideas and issues
- **skills (S)** — the use of language (grammar, spelling and punctuation — GSP) and logic, as well as geographical skills such as maps and diagrams

In many cases, the above criteria are assessed at one of four levels. In general terms, these levels can be summarised as follows:

Level I

K — generalised material; no or limited case studies or just simple statements of examples; inappropriate or incorrect use of terms; irrelevance

U — weak grasp of concepts and ideas; description only

S — basic; not always logical; clear expression of simple ideas

Level II

K — some use of case studies but a lack of depth and detail

U — some understanding of processes by explanation; some evidence of evaluation

S — some illustrative material; logical; GSP is satisfactory, accurate use of English

Level III

K — good use of case studies; appropriate and detailed; good locational knowledge

U — good understanding of processes and issues; evaluative comment

S — a logical and coherent argument; the essay is said to 'flow'; almost faultless accuracy in the use of English

Level IV

This may occur in some essay questions when some overall evaluation of a concept or of an issue is required, often in response to the higher-level command 'discuss'. Candidates who have the ability to synthesise and draw together their argument(s) will access this level and gain very high marks.

Content
Guidance

The content of **Module 4: Global Change** falls into three main areas:

Physical geography
This involves the study of:
- the pattern and causes of seasonal atmospheric changes at a global scale
- seasonal changes within the tropical regions of Africa with wet and dry seasons and the influence on hydrology and ecology
- long-term climatic change
- changing vegetation and soils in the British Isles
- the relationship between the global structures and processes of the Earth's surface
- the location of tectonic processes and the consequences of such processes

People and the environment
This involves the study of:
- hazards (burglary, transmittable disease, tropical storms, volcanoes, earthquakes and a case study of one major urban area with multiple hazards)
- the origin, distribution, frequency, scale and effects of hazards
- the extent to which hazards can be predicted and/or prevented
- types of response to hazards, including management and relief
- competition and conflict over the use of a resource at a local scale

Human geography
This involves the study of:
- transnational corporations (TNCs) and the global economy
- the relationship between international migration and multicultural societies
- the extent to which regions of a country are integrated or subject to separatist pressures
- the extent to which political power within groups of nations is centralised or decentralised, and the consequences of this
- development issues within an LEDC or MEDC (excluding the UK)

Physical geography

The pattern and causes of seasonal atmospheric changes

The general atmospheric circulation system

The general atmospheric circulation system is shown in the diagram below. It shows three circular movements of air, called **cells**, in each hemisphere. The three cells are called the Hadley cell, the Ferrel cell and the polar cell.

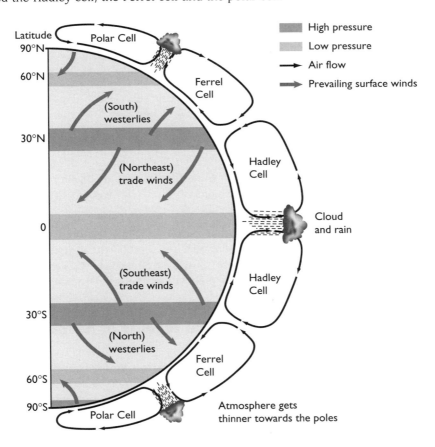

The Hadley cell is largely responsible for the seasonal changes in tropical regions of Africa with wet and dry seasons (see page 12). It has four sections:

- the area of low pressure in equatorial latitudes, also known as the inter-tropical convergence zone (ITCZ). With the sun always high in the sky, the ground near the equator becomes very hot and water on the surface evaporates. The hot air and water vapour rise in convection currents and an area of low pressure develops. As the rising air cools, the water vapour condenses to give heavy rain.
- the poleward movement of air at high altitudes. The air that has risen moves in a

poleward direction, both north and south of the equator. In most cases, this air circulates as upper westerly winds around the planet due to the deflection effect of the rotation of the Earth, known as the Coriolis effect, but the net effect is that the air still moves polewards.

- the areas of high pressure at 30°N and 30°S — the subtropical anticyclones. Some of the colder air at high altitude begins to sink, or subside, back to the surface. As this air descends, it warms and evaporates any residual moisture. An area of high pressure is created at the ground surface, which generally means cloudless skies.
- the areas of trade winds. On reaching the ground at the subtropical anticyclones, some of the air returns to the equatorial latitudes as consistent winds. These movements of air from both north and south of the equator are also affected by the Coriolis effect, and are deflected to the right in the northern hemisphere and to the left in the southern hemisphere. Hence, the northeast trades blow north of the equator and the southeast trades blow south of the equator.

The position of these four sections varies through the year. Due to the tilt of the Earth, the position of the overhead sun moves between seasons. On June 21, the sun is overhead at the Tropic of Cancer, and so the whole pressure pattern and winds move north of the equator. On December 21, the sun is overhead at the Tropic of Capricorn, and the pressure pattern and winds move south of the equator. It is this seasonal change in pressure, and the resultant winds, that is responsible for the seasonal changes in the climate of the tropical regions of Africa with wet and dry seasons (see below).

Some geographers believe that the system described above is due more to the convergence (or meeting) of air from the trade winds, and its subsequent rise, in equatorial latitudes than to the apparent movement of the overhead sun. Consequently, most now refer to the equatorial area of low pressure as the inter-tropical convergence zone (ITCZ).

Seasonal changes within tropical regions of Africa with wet and dry seasons

Seasonal variations in wind direction, precipitation and temperature

The climate of the tropical regions of Africa with wet and dry seasons is transitional between the equatorial rainforests and the hot deserts, and variations occur with increasing latitude. However, all areas are characterised by having a dry season (little or no rain) and a wet season (when up to 90% of the annual rainfall falls).

At the rainforest margins:
- precipitation is over 1000 mm per year with one or two dry months
- the temperature ranges from 24 °C in the wet season to 28 °C in the dry season

At the desert or semi-arid margins:
- precipitation is under 500 mm per year with nine or ten dry months, and the reliability of the rainfall decreases with increasing latitude
- the temperature ranges from 18 °C in the wet season to 34 °C in the dry season

During the dry season, the subtropical anticyclone moves over the desert margins of the area. The ITCZ is on the equatorial side. Hence, these areas are affected by trade winds blowing from the land towards the coasts (offshore) and by relatively high pressure. The subsiding air gives clear skies and high daytime temperatures, and convection is suppressed. In the case of north Africa, dry tropical continental air (called the Harmattan), with a very low moisture content, often blows from the hot Sahara desert.

During the wet season, the ITCZ migrates polewards. As it moves, it brings rainfall. Uplift and convection are fed by moist, unstable, tropical maritime air. Areas at the poleward limit of the ITCZ are only briefly affected, and thus have a short wet season and low annual rainfall totals. Nearer the equator, the wet season lasts while the ITCZ has moved polewards; such areas have longer periods of rain and higher totals. Maximum precipitation occurs with the actual passage polewards of the ITCZ and on its return, thus giving a double maximum of rainfall in some areas.

For the discussion that follows, a northern hemisphere weather pattern is assumed. This means that in an area such as northern Ghana, the wet season occurs between May and September and the dry season occurs between October and April.

Hydrological responses to seasonal atmospheric changes

There is a pronounced peak in the discharge of rivers during the late summer months of August to October. This corresponds not only to the heavy rainfall at this time but more specifically to the period of water surplus in the soil moisture budget (see below). The spell of maximum precipitation in June to August, the soil moisture recharge, does not lead immediately to an increase in the discharge. Discharge reduces rapidly during the onset of the dry season and remains low from November to May, during the water deficit period. The minimum discharge occurs soon after the period of highest temperatures — the time of peak evapotranspiration.

Ecological responses to seasonal atmospheric changes
Soil moisture budgets

The diagram overleaf shows a typical soil moisture graph for a location in northern Ghana (Navrongo) which experiences a climate with wet and dry seasons. Precipitation is greater than potential evapotranspiration between July and September, whereas potential evapotranspiration is greater than precipitation between October and June.

When precipitation is greater than potential evapotranspiration, at first there is some refilling of water into the pores within the dry soil. This is **soil moisture recharge**. When the soil is saturated, excess water has difficulty infiltrating into the ground, and may flow over the surface. This is **soil moisture surplus**.

When potential evapotranspiration is greater than precipitation, water evaporates from the ground surface and transpires from plants. Water may also be brought up to the surface through capillary action and then evaporate. This is **soil moisture utilisation**. However, eventually the soil will dry out completely, creating a **soil moisture deficit**.

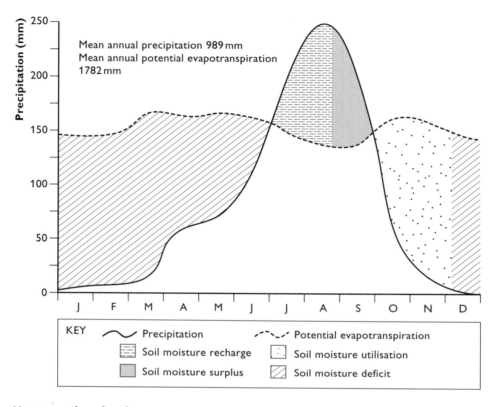

Mean annual precipitation 989 mm
Mean annual potential evapotranspiration 1782 mm

KEY

~ Precipitation   ⌒⌣⌒ Potential evapotranspiration

Soil moisture recharge   Soil moisture utilisation

Soil moisture surplus   Soil moisture deficit

Navrongo therefore has:

- a lengthy period of moisture deficit and a short period of moisture surplus
- total annual potential evapotranspiration greater than total annual precipitation

Adaptations by vegetation

The vegetation in wetter areas consists of tall, coarse grasses (elephant grass) with many trees which are usually deciduous. This is known as the tree savanna. In drier areas towards the desert margins, shorter tussock grass appears with bare soil between the tufts of grass, often accompanied by drought-resistant trees such as the acacia and the baobab. These are known as the grassland and scrub savannas.

Most trees are deciduous, losing their leaves in the dry season, although some evergreens are also found. Their hard leathery leaves reduce transpiration losses, while some plants may be microphyllous (small-leaved) to reduce transpiration. In the tree savanna, a parkland exists — isolated trees with low, umbrella-shaped crowns shade root areas and thus reduce soil moisture evaporation. The trees show xerophytic characteristics, with dense cell fluids, hard waxy leaves, thorns and protected stomata, which all reduce water loss. The acacia trees lose their leaves in the dry season. The baobab, with its thick spongy trunk, insulative bark and long tap roots, bears leaves for only a few weeks. All these features reduce water loss.

In the grassland savanna, the grasses between the trees becomes shorter and sparser. They are perennial — dying back during the dry season and then regrowing from root nodules in the wet season. The grasses are tussocky, enabling some retention of moisture. The naturally created straw dies down and protects roots.

In the scrub savanna, there are mainly acacia trees, thorn bushes and short, tufted grasses. Many species generate short stems from a single stock, with deep branched roots and dormant seeds which compete for water. In some plants, even the stems may be capable of photosynthesis. Some grasses are feathery and wiry, and turn their blades away from the strong sun, which reduces water loss.

The effects of human activity on vegetation

Human activity has two main effects on the vegetation of these areas:

- Grass is burned off to ensure better growth of young grass in subsequent seasons. When fire sweeps through vegetation at frequent intervals, it is very difficult for young trees and bushes to become established. Their place is taken by herbaceous plants and by the few indigenous woody plants whose bark permits them to survive. Examples of these include the acacia and the baobab. Consequently, these trees are common.
- In areas where grazing cattle are numerous, woody plants are killed by the removal of their foliage. Thorny, animal-repellent trees and shrubs, such as acacias, have therefore become numerous.

Some geographers believe that these activities have had a greater influence than the climate on the development of the vegetation of such areas.

Long-term climatic change

The climate of the British Isles has changed significantly since the Pleistocene Ice Age ended about 10 000 years ago. The climatic warming that began at the end of the ice age was the start of a trend that has continued to the present day. This general trend has been interrupted by brief periods of cooling.

Evidence for climatic change

Evidence from a variety of sources can be used to reconstruct changes in past climates. Most of this evidence is *indirect* (or proxy evidence); change in climate is inferred from changes in other indicators that reflect climate.

Geomorphological evidence

Field study and analysis of areas in the British Isles indicate that glacial landforms and sediment deposits were eroded or laid down under conditions and processes that are not active at the present time. Changes in sea level have occurred due to the melting of ice sheets; isostatic uplift has produced raised beaches in some areas; a eustatic rise of sea level has caused the submergence of lower sections of river valleys and glacial troughs, to form rias and fjords.

Sea floor evidence

Emiliani measured the level of oxygen isotopes in fossils taken from mud cores from the ocean floor. With increasing depth in a core, the sediments revealed shifts of animal and plant populations from warmer to colder forms. The ratio of the isotopes oxygen-18 to oxygen-16 in calcareous ooze varied in a similar pattern. During colder phases, when water is evaporated from the oceans and precipitated on the land to form glacial ice, water containing lighter oxygen-16 is more easily evaporated than that containing heavier oxygen-18. As a result, the oceans have a concentration of oxygen-18 while glaciers contain more of the lighter oxygen-16. During warmer periods, the oxygen-16 held in glacial ice is released and returns to the oceans to balance the ratio. Therefore, studies of isotope curves showing the ratio of oxygen-16 to oxygen-18 give a generalised view of climatic change. More recent studies suggest that isotope variations are an indication of changes in the volume of ice contained within ice sheets and glaciers rather than water temperature; but ice volume would also reflect climatic conditions.

Ice core analysis

The study of carbon dioxide concentrations in air bubbles trapped in glacial ice has revealed evidence of climatic change. Carbon dioxide concentrations correspond with other indicators; values were low during colder periods and higher during warmer phases.

Pollen analysis

Many plant species have particular climatic requirements which influence their geographical distribution. Pollen grains can be used to determine the vegetation changes and, by implication, the changes in climatic conditions.

Dendrochronology

Trees record climatic conditions through growth rates. Each year, a tree produces a growth ring made up of two bands: a band reflecting rapid spring growth when the cells are larger, and a narrower band of growth during the cooler autumn or winter. The width of the tree ring indicates the conditions that prevailed during its growth cycle, a wider ring indicating a warmer period. The change in ring width from year to year is more significant than the actual width because bigger growth rings tend to be produced during the early years of growth, irrespective of the weather. It is possible to match and overlap samples from different sources, for example from living trees and from beams from older houses, to extend dating back in time.

Documentary evidence

Diaries, written accounts, lithographs and paintings can all be used to study climatic conditions in the recent (historic) period. Frost fairs were held on the River Thames in the seventeenth century and these are well documented as an indication that conditions were more severe than at the present time.

Meteorological data, in the form of daily weather reports, are available for the British Isles from 1873 onwards, although the Royal Society had encouraged the collection of weather data from the 1660s.

Accurate, direct evidence of weather and climatic change is therefore very recent in terms of post-Pleistocene change; evidence for earlier periods can only be indirect.

The following table shows the main climatic periods during the last 10 000 years.

Climatic period	Time before present	Climatic conditions	Mean temperature change (°C) +1 0 −1 −2 −3 −4 −5
Sub-Atlantic	2500	• A period of warming in the last 200 years • Temperatures fluctuate; cooler than the present day • A cool coastal climate with cooler summers and increased rainfall • A marked cool period between AD 1300 and AD 1800 — the Little Ice Age	
Sub-Boreal	5000	• Temperatures falling but rainfall relatively low at the beginning of this period, increasing later • Period known as the neoglacial period in Europe, with evidence of ice advance in Alpine areas • Warm summers and colder winters	
Atlantic	7500	• Temperatures reach the optimum for many trees and shrubs — the 'climatic optimum' • A warm 'west coast' type of climate, with higher rainfall	
Boreal	9000	• Climate becoming warmer and drier • A continental-type climate	
Pre-Boreal	10 300	• Mainly cold and wet, but becoming warmer and drier • Changing from Tundra/sub-Arctic to more continental	

Recent global warming

Evidence for global warming comes from climatic data and the fact that glaciers and ice sheets are thinning or receding.

Carbon dioxide allows incoming short-wave radiation to pass through, but it absorbs some of the long-wave radiation emitted from Earth to space. Provided that the amount of carbon dioxide and water vapour in the atmosphere are not altered and the amount of solar radiation is unchanged, then the temperature of the Earth remains in balance. Incoming radiation is absorbed by the Earth's surface and the lower atmosphere (the troposphere), and some heat is re-radiated from the Earth to warm the troposphere. The troposphere also radiates heat towards the ground. This is known as the greenhouse effect and is part of the natural process of heat balance in the atmosphere. However, this natural balance has been influenced by human activity. The atmospheric concentration of carbon dioxide has increased by about 15% in the last 100 years and the current rate of increase in carbon dioxide is estimated at 0.4% per year. Increases in carbon dioxide, largely the result of burning fossil fuels which contain hydrocarbons, together with other greenhouse gases such as methane, nitrous oxide and CFCs, have upset the natural balance and this has led to global warming. The global temperature change over the last century has been about 5 °C, although this may have been influenced by other environmental factors, such as volcanic activity and changes in circulation of ocean currents.

It is generally agreed that the changes will cause a further rise in temperature, but it is difficult to predict the extent or speed of change. A further doubling of carbon dioxide levels could raise surface temperatures by as much as 2–3 °C, with greater warming in the higher latitudes — perhaps by as much as 7–8 °C.

These changes have serious implications for climate patterns, sea levels and economic activity. The variation in heating effect could influence the pattern of air circulation and prevailing winds and therefore change seasonal patterns of rainfall and extreme forms of weather. Warmer oceans result in greater levels of moisture in tropical storms, leading to a release of energy in hurricanes and cyclones and more severe rainfall. Changes in circulation could cause continental areas to become drier, influencing the agriculture and human food supply in these areas. Sea levels are likely to change because of the expansion of the oceans as a result of higher water temperatures and a decrease in ice held on land masses. Areas undergoing pressure release as a result of the removal of ice could experience sea level falls, whereas the melting of ice caps and glaciers would produce a eustatic rise in sea level, which would have serious effects upon low-lying coastal areas. The extent of sea level rise is not known. Estimates suggest that it could be as much as 60 cm by AD 2030; the most extreme view is that the level could rise by 5 m by AD 2050.

Changing vegetation and soils in the British Isles

Vegetation succession and climax vegetation

The composition of vegetation depends on the interaction between all the components of the environment in which the plants live — the habitat. Plants will survive where conditions are suitable; environmental factors and competition affect this. Plant populations vary from one area to another and also change with *time*; communities generally become more complex.

This change through time is called **succession**. If the development begins on ground on which there has been no previous vegetation (for example a lava flow, bare rock surface or sand dune system), then it is termed a **primary succession**. If the succession is initiated by the destruction or modification of pre-existing vegetation, either naturally or by human activity, then it is termed **secondary succession**.

As the succession develops, it passes through a series of stages, or **seres**, in which the processes of invasion, colonisation, competition, domination and decline operate to influence the composition of the vegetation.

When plants first invade bare ground through their usual process of dispersion or migration, a number of groups of a particular species, or colonies of two or more species, become established. These **pioneer** species compete for available space, light, water and nutrients. As they die, they help to modify the existing habitat, affecting the microclimate (wind speed, shelter, temperature range near the ground, humidity) and soil conditions (organic content, nutrient recycling, acidity, water retention). Plants also help to weather the surface and so aid soil formation.

Other plants arrive from neighbouring areas to colonise the ground; these in turn affect the existing balance. Each stage produces a more welcoming environment for a wider variety of species. New dominants take over and exert their own influence. Colonisation initiates succession as the addition of organic matter allows the growth of other plants that are more demanding of water, nutrients and anchorage — taller, more aggressive, species. Shelter and protection allow other plants to become established.

Eventually, a period of relative stability is achieved. The **climax vegetation** develops, with dominants excluding rivals that are less suited to the conditions. Generally, as time progresses, the number of species increases through to domination, but once the major dominants are in place they may cause a decline in the number of species. Climax is usually dominated by the tallest species that can become established in the area. The system reaches 'saturation point' in terms of the number of species. The community is 'closed'; all potential niches are occupied and the progression is at an end. An uninterrupted succession produces a **climatic climax community**.

An example of primary succession — a lithosere

A lithosere takes place on a newly exposed bare rock surface. This surface may have been exposed by the retreat of an ice sheet or as a result of landslips and scree formation. An example of a lithosere in the British Isles would be as follows:

- The bare rock surface would initially be colonised by bacteria and algae, which can survive where there are few nutrients; the bare rock is very arid because there is rapid surface run-off.
- Pioneer species such as lichens (able to withstand acute water shortage) colonise the surface. They assist in weathering the rock and improve water retention.

- Once water retention improves, then mosses are able to colonise. These also aid water retention and weathering to form a thin layer of soil in which more advanced plants can grow.
- Grasses, ferns, herbs and flowering plants colonise. As these die back, bacteria convert their remains into humus, which helps to recycle nutrients and further improve soil fertility.
- Shrubs colonise, which in turn begin to reduce grass cover by competition for light.
- Pioneer trees move in. These are mainly fast-growing species such as willow, birch, and rowan.
- Slower-growing species such as ash and oak develop. Initially, these species are in the shade of the shrubs, so they only appear in the later stages of the succession. They form the dominants in the climax community: temperate deciduous woodland. Stratification of the vegetation is evident, with a field and shrub layer beneath the tree canopy layer.

Evidence used to identify changes in vegetation

Pollen grains are frequently used as indicators of previous vegetation distribution and past climate. Most plant species have particular requirements for growth and, assuming that these requirements have not changed, it is possible to determine the pattern of vegetation, and therefore the characteristics of the climate, in the past.

Pollen grains are particularly useful for research because of the following properties:
- Seed-bearing, higher species of plant produce pollen grains and lower species of plant produce spores in large amounts; they are therefore widely available for analysis.
- Pollen grains for each species have distinctive structures.
- Pollen grains are resistant to decomposition if deposited in an environment where oxidation is restricted. Suitable environments for preservation are peat bogs, lake floors and sea floor sediments.
- Pollen grains are deposited in layers in these sediments. If these are undisturbed, then the pollen grains are deposited in sequence, with the oldest pollen at greater depth. As samples are taken down through the sediment, changes over time can be identified.
- A vertical sequence of samples can be collected by making a borehole through a preservation site, or using a peat borer. Each sample can then be analysed for pollen and spore content. Pollen grains can be counted under a high-power microscope and a pollen diagram can be constructed to show the percentage representation of each type of pollen.
- Modern methods of dating materials, such as carbon-14 dating, allow specific dates to be added to the sequence of vegetation changes shown by pollen analysis.

The effects of human activity on vegetation successions

Human influences can stop a succession from reaching the climatic climax vegetation, or deflect the succession towards a different climax — producing a **plagioclimax** vegetation. Deforestation, animal grazing, fire/clearance and trampling can all arrest a succession and cause it to be altered. In the British Isles, heather now dominates uplands that were once forested. Heather would have occurred naturally, but in smaller amounts. Present dominance has been encouraged and maintained by deforestation and managed burning which has eliminated less fire-resistant species. Sheep grazing has prevented the regeneration of climax woodland as the animals destroy the young saplings. In other areas, heather has invaded surfaces where the removal of oak and birch woodland has led to increased soil erosion through leaching and a rise in acidity, which has restricted the regrowth of trees. Much of the present-day vegetation of the British Isles is a plagioclimax, largely as a result of clearance from the Roman and Anglo-Saxon periods through to the eleventh century, when only about 10% of woodland remained in England and Wales.

Soil characteristics

The characteristics and properties of a soil are the result of interactions between a number of factors: climate, organic material (from vegetation), relief, parent material and time. The nature of a soil changes through time as it develops from an immature skeletal soil to one that is developed fully and in balance with its environment. In addition, human activity can have an important impact on the soil.

Environmental factors produce the main components of the soil — water, air, mineral matter and organic material. The interrelationships between these components result in 'soil characteristics' or properties.

Mineral constituents

Mineral constituents are produced by weathering of the underlying parent material. They are the products of both physical breakdown (such as freeze–thaw) and chemical attack (for example, oxidation, carbonation and hydrolysis). These weathering products can be divided into two groups:
- **Primary minerals** remain unaltered from the original parent material. They are simply released from the parent material by weathering. Primary minerals are almost insoluble and make up the inorganic fraction in the soil.
- **Secondary minerals** are produced in the soil by chemical reactions. They are readily soluble and are predominantly carbonates, because weak carbonic acid is an input to soils as precipitation. Although weak, the carbonic acid can detach potassium, magnesium and calcium from the parent material in the form of carbonates: K_2CO_3, $MgCO_3$, $Ca(HCO_3)_2$.

Chemical weathering generally produces clay compounds. Even with resistant rocks (e.g. granite), potassium, magnesium and carbonates are released, together with sesquioxides of iron and aluminium. Quartz is released as sand grains when the parent material disintegrates. The sand and clay make up the inorganic fraction; the soluble products enter the soil. A **sesquioxide**, such as Al_2O_3 (aluminium sesquioxide), has three oxygen atoms to two aluminium atoms.

Particle size

The composition of the parent material will influence the constituents in the soil and the particle size. Particle size is an important property because it influences texture, which in turn affects structure, availability of pore space, and water and nutrient retention.

Texture is the distribution of grain sizes within the soil mineral component. This relates only to the fine earth fraction — particles less than 2 mm in diameter — which is divided into three major groups:

- sand, 0.06–2 mm (60–2000 microns) diameter
- silt, 0.002–0.06 mm (2–60 microns)
- clay, less than 0.002 mm (<2 microns)

Analysis of texture involves assessing the percentage of sand, silt and clay fractions. This is conventionally represented by means of a triangular graph. Soils with a high sand content usually have a weak structure. The coarser particles provide a large amount of air space but lead to rapid drainage of water and poor nutrient retention capacity. Minerals are easily leached through sandy soils. Clay soils have a much greater surface area available for nutrient retention but drainage is impeded. They are often heavy to plough, and plant root penetration is difficult. Clay soils become waterlogged easily, and shrink on drying. Silty soils often have low organic retention and are open to erosion and waterlogging.

High concentrations of sand, silt or clay create problems for agricultural use. The ideal soil has a mixture of sand, silt and clay, as this combines the good properties of each particle size. A loamy soil has a clay component to retain soil moisture and nutrients, a sand component to aid drainage and reduce the risk of waterlogging, and a silt fraction which helps to bind the sand and clay together.

Structure is the way in which the individual particles are arranged or grouped together. The aggregation of particles forms **peds**. This grouping is encouraged by the incorporation of organic matter and gums and mucilages produced during bacterial breakdown, which help to bind the peds together. Spaces between peds allow the passage of water and soil microfauna.

The texture and structure influence the amount of space between the soil particles and peds for retention of water and aeration. Clays have a large number of small pores (micropores) whereas sands have larger pores (macropores) which allow water to pass through more quickly. A loam provides a balance of pore sizes.

If all the pore spaces are filled with water, then there is no space for air within the soil; this is termed an **anaerobic** state. As the soil water drains under gravity, the water vacates the larger cavities. When the soil has lost this gravitational water, it is described as being at **field capacity**. Gravitational water is of little value to plants as it drains away quickly after rainfall input. At field capacity, water is still held in the finer pores as hygroscopic water and capillary water. Hygroscopic water is tightly bonded to the soil particles at pressures up to 10 000 atmospheres. It is not available to plants and can only be removed from soil at high temperatures under laboratory conditions. Capillary water can rise vertically to about 1m above the water table. This water is available to plants, but is lost from the soil by transpiration and evaporation. When there is no longer sufficient water in the soil to meet the transpiration demands of plants, the soil is at **wilting point**, and plants will suffer stress.

Pores not occupied by water contain air, which is essential for plant growth and organisms within the soil.

Types of humus

When plant organs die, they undergo initial decay and disintegration as bacteria and fungi break down the leaf litter (and faecal remains from animals). As the organic matter decays, the leaf debris is no longer recognisable and humus is produced. When the organic material can be identified as a distinct layer on the top of the soil, it is termed **discrete humus**. As humification continues, this humus becomes incorporated into the soil as **intimate humus**, forming an essential part of the clay–humus complex.

Three distinct types of discrete humus can be recognised. Each reflects the environment and nutrient cycle operating in the area where it is formed. Some plants take up more minerals, such as potassium and calcium, and incorporate them into their leaves. Consequently, their plant organs are rich in nutrients. When they decay, the nutrients are returned to the soil and become incorporated in the humus. This produces a neutral or mildly acidic humus, **mull**, which is soft, blackish and crumbly. It is commonly found in lowland areas of hardwoods and grasslands. Under more acidic conditions, for example on upland heath and bog areas, where breakdown is slower, the plants take up, and hence return, fewer nutrients. This produces a raw, fibrous, acid humus called **mor**. Finally, a transitional mor-like mull, or **moder**, can be distinguished.

Plant nutrients and ionic exchange

Nutrients are elements found in the soil that are essential for plant growth. There are three main sources of nutrients in the soil:

- Nutrients dissolved in the soil water are available to plants but are easily removed by the loss of gravitational water.
- Humus compounds and micelles of clay undergo chemical linkage to form clay–humus complexes. These complexes are capable of retaining mineral elements in an exchangeable form (cation exchange). Nutrients are attached (adsorbed) to the clay–humus complex and this acts as the most important store of minerals within the soil.
- Nutrients are also stored in minerals within the inorganic fraction in the soil but these are unavailable to plants unless weathering releases them and they are dissolved in soil water.

If the clay–humus complex were not present, then rainwater would easily remove all the soluble salts from the soil. Inorganic salts, when dissolved in water, ionise to a considerable extent. For example, dissolved molecules of potassium carbonate in soil solution are partly dissociated into potassium ions and carbonate ions:

$$K_2CO_3 \longrightarrow K^+ + K^+ + CO_3^-$$

Each of the free potassium ions carries a positive charge with which it is able to relink with the carbonate ion or with any other similar ion in the soil. The particles of clay and humus develop negatively charged ions (anions). The negatively charged clay–humus complex therefore attracts the positively charged potassium ion. These mineral ions develop loose temporary linkages with the clay–humus micelle. Other minerals (magnesium, calcium, ammonium and sodium) and hydrogen can be retained in a similar way.

The nutrients adsorbed to the clay–humus complex become detached and can be absorbed as food by plant roots. Cations of calcium, potassium and magnesium are released and replace an equal number of hydrogen cations which were initially attached to the plant roots. The plants obtain essential nutrients by exchanging hydrogen ions for the nutrients adsorbed to the clay–humus complex.

Different soils have different cation exchange capacities, i.e. the ability to store nutrients. Clearly, a soil consisting of a mixture of sand and silt cannot be fertile — the nutrients will be too easily removed. Soils need a clay component to develop their nutrient retention capacity.

Soil pH
The number of exchangeable mineral ions in a soil is a measure of its base status. Soil pH relates to the number of hydrogen ions in the soil — the greater the concentration of hydrogen ions, the more acidic the soil.

The lower the hydrogen ion concentration, the higher the pH (i.e. more alkaline). As it is a logarithmic relationship, pH 1 is ten times more acidic (i.e. has ten times the level of hydrogen ion concentration) than pH 2. In terms of soil chemistry, the pH scale ranges from 1 to 14, with a reading of 7 being neutral.

Soil processes and profiles
The characteristics of soil profiles reflect the interaction between processes operating in that particular environment. The most commonly used system of horizon notation divides a soil into three basic units:
- **A** — the mineral and organic layer near the surface; a zone of eluviation which may lose soluble salts by drainage and downwash
- **B** — the subsurface horizon of illuviation, in which accumulation of material from A occurs
- **C** — the mineral matter of geological origin, in which the horizons are forming; the weathered parent material or regolith

Other letters are used to denote other surface and subsurface zones.

Surface horizons	L	Leaf; undecomposed litter
	F	Partially decomposed; fermentation layer
	H	Well decomposed; humus layer
A	Ah	Dark-coloured humic horizon
	Ap	Ploughed layer in cultivated soils
	E	Eluvial horizon from which clay/sesquioxides have been removed
	Ea	Bleached (albic or ash-like) layer in podzolised soils
	Eb	Brown eluvial layer, depleted of clay

	Bt	Illuvial clay redeposited (textural B horizon)
B	Bh	Illuvial humus layer
	Bf/Bfe	Illuviated iron layer
	Bs	Brightly coloured layer of sesquioxide (iron/aluminium) accumulation
C		Weathered parent material

This is illustrated in the following profile, which is that of a brown earth soil.

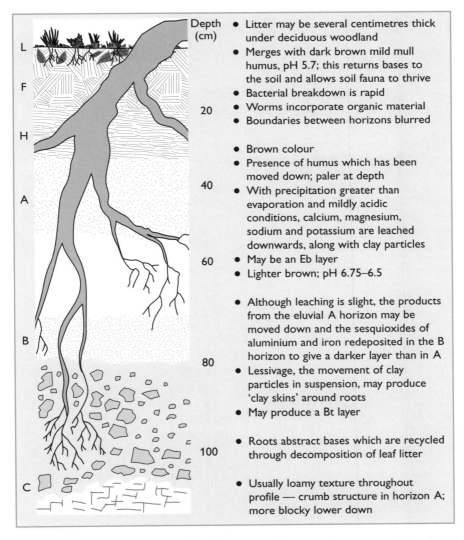

Depth (cm)

L
- Litter may be several centimetres thick under deciduous woodland
F
- Merges with dark brown mild mull humus, pH 5.7; this returns bases to the soil and allows soil fauna to thrive
- Bacterial breakdown is rapid
20
- Worms incorporate organic material
H
- Boundaries between horizons blurred

A
- Brown colour
- Presence of humus which has been moved down; paler at depth
40
- With precipitation greater than evaporation and mildly acidic conditions, calcium, magnesium, sodium and potassium are leached downwards, along with clay particles
60
- May be an Eb layer
- Lighter brown; pH 6.75–6.5

B
- Although leaching is slight, the products from the eluvial A horizon may be moved down and the sesquioxides of aluminium and iron redeposited in the B horizon to give a darker layer than in A
80
- Lessivage, the movement of clay particles in suspension, may produce 'clay skins' around roots
- May produce a Bt layer

100
- Roots abstract bases which are recycled through decomposition of leaf litter

C
- Usually loamy texture throughout profile — crumb structure in horizon A; more blocky lower down

In the British Isles, where precipitation generally exceeds evaporation, there is predominantly a downward movement of water in the soil. The main processes involved are **leaching** and **podzolisation**, which occur in soils that allow free drainage

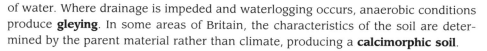

of water. Where drainage is impeded and waterlogging occurs, anaerobic conditions produce **gleying**. In some areas of Britain, the characteristics of the soil are determined by the parent material rather than climate, producing a **calcimorphic soil**.

Leaching

Leaching is the downward movement of material in solution or in colloidal suspension. Rainwater, which is a weak carbonic acid, combines with organic acids produced by the breakdown of organic material at the surface to produce a complex acid solution which causes chemical breakdown in the soil. Soluble bases are dissolved and carried down through the soil profile. Clay particles may be moved down through the profile in suspension — a process of eluviation known as lessivage.

These processes are illustrated in the profile of a **brown earth soil** (see page 25).

Podzolisation

Podzolisation (cheluviation) is a more intense form of leaching which operates under more acidic conditions. A **podzol soil** profile is illustrated below.

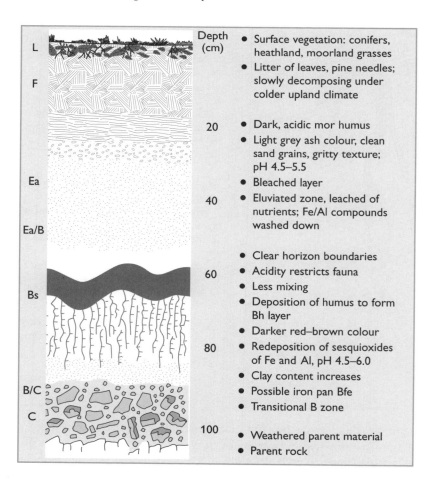

Stronger humic acids, or chelating agents, are released as a result of the slower break-down of the more acidic raw humus (mor) produced under coniferous woodland and upland heaths. Aluminium and iron sesquioxides are unstable under these acidic conditions and are moved down through the profile leaving a bleached, silica-rich, sandy layer in the A horizon. The aluminium and iron compounds are redeposited in the B horizon and the iron deposits may accumulate to form an iron pan.

Gleying

Gleying occurs when water movement through the soil is restricted. This may be caused either by a high water table (groundwater gley) or as a result of an imper-meable layer within the soil which impedes the movement of water (surface water gley). This impermeable layer may be caused by soil processes. For example, the formation of an iron pan within a podzol restricts water movement at depth. This can produce a gleyed layer above the iron pan. A **gley soil** profile is illustrated below.

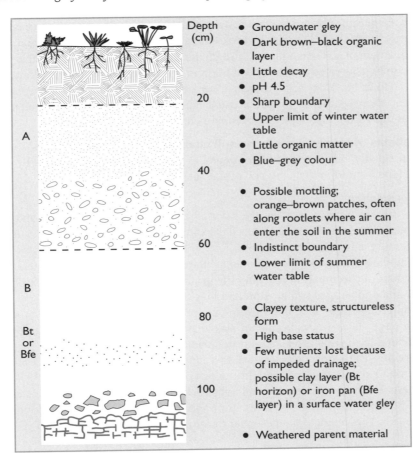

Depth (cm)	
	• Groundwater gley
	• Dark brown–black organic layer
	• Little decay
	• pH 4.5
20	• Sharp boundary
	• Upper limit of winter water table
	• Little organic matter
	• Blue–grey colour
40	
	• Possible mottling; orange–brown patches, often along rootlets where air can enter the soil in the summer
60	• Indistinct boundary
	• Lower limit of summer water table
80	• Clayey texture, structureless form
	• High base status
	• Few nutrients lost because of impeded drainage; possible clay layer (Bt horizon) or iron pan (Bfe layer) in a surface water gley
100	
	• Weathered parent material

Groundwater gleys are usually associated with low-lying areas such as valley floors. Under waterlogged conditions, all the pore spaces are occupied by water, producing anaerobic (oxygen-deficient) conditions. Under these conditions, the decomposition of plant debris on the surface is slow and the presence of organic matter and specialised bacteria cause reducing conditions under which the solubility of many constituents is changed. Iron, which is relatively insoluble in its ferric (oxidised) form over the normal range of soil pH, is much more soluble when reduced to the ferrous form. Under waterlogged conditions, iron becomes more mobile and is slowly removed from the system. The gleyed soil is a bluish-grey colour. Often, the water-logging is seasonal as the height of the water table varies. This leads to mottling, with orange–brown coloration produced when oxygen enters the soil and oxidation occurs.

Calcimorphic soils

A calcimorphic soil, or **rendzina**, is an example of an intrazonal soil — one that develops on a particular rock type rather than under certain climatic conditions. Rendzinas develop on a parent material of chalk or limestone. Where grasses are the surface vegetation, the leaf litter is rich in bases which produce a less acidic mull humus, favourable for microfaunal activity. This produces rapid recycling of nutrients. The presence of the calcium-rich clays and the calcium carbonate in the soil restricts the movement of soil constituents through the formation of chemically stable calcium compounds. Therefore, there is no B horizon. These soils are rich in organic matter and tend to be black or dark red–brown. Because the parent material produces soluble residues when weathered, the soil is usually quite shallow and has a low soil moisture content due to the underlying permeable bedrock.

The effects of human activity on soil characteristics and profiles

Human activity can either damage (degrade) or improve (upgrade) soils by altering characteristics and influencing soil processes.

Soil degradation

- Harvesting of crops removes the natural supply of recycled nutrients and organic material. These need to be replaced through the use of natural or artificial fertilisers if fertility is to be maintained.
- Removing vegetation, for example by deforestation or overgrazing, increases the amount of precipitation reaching the ground surface. This increases surface run-off and encourages soil erosion and loss of nutrients.
- Ploughing under wet conditions can produce a plough pan which restricts drainage. It can also break up stable peds and loosen soil, making it more vulnerable to wind erosion, with the resultant loss of nutrients.
- Growing the same crop year after year (monoculture) causes a depletion of nutrients at a particular depth in the soil profile.
- The use of heavy machinery and overstocking causes compaction. This creates a platy structure which impedes drainage and could lead to waterlogging and gleying. This restricts the potential for crop production.

Soil improvement (conservation)

- Adding fertiliser, either NPK or farmyard manure (FYM), improves nutrient content. Organic fertiliser (FYM) increases the input of organic material from crop residues and organic waste. This encourages soil organisms and improves nutrient retention through the development of the clay–humus complex.

- Growing vegetation — cover crops or afforestation — helps to stabilise the soil and return leaf litter, providing a longer-term solution to soil erosion.
- Improved farming methods influence soils. For example:
  - crop rotation/fallow periods allow soil to replenish nutrients
  - shelter belts reduce the impact of wind erosion
  - improving field drainage lowers the water table and increases aeration
  - liming raises the pH, improves soil structure and increases the availability of calcium as a nutrient for plants and an encouragement for soil organisms
  - cultivation and drainage improve structure by breaking up peds, creating a crumb structure and increasing pore space
  - mulching (the addition of organic material to the soil), for example ploughing in stubble, increases the organic content and improves the retention of nutrients
  - ploughing helps to aerate the soil and break up peds; deep ploughing can improve overall soil drainage, which is beneficial in poorly drained areas if undertaken at the right time

Plate tectonics

Theory of plate tectonics

Plate tectonics is the name given to a set of concepts or theories that explain the formation and distribution of the Earth's major structural features by reference to the relative movement of plates which make up the Earth's surface. These structural features include continents, ocean basins, mountain ranges, trenches and volcanoes.

Before the development of plate tectonic theory in the 1960s, earth scientists divided the Earth's interior into three layers — the crust, the mantle and the core — based upon chemical differences. The **core**, made up of dense rocks (density 12) containing iron and nickel alloys, has a solid inner core and molten outer zone, with a temperature of approximately 5500 °C. The **mantle**, with a density of 5.7 near the core, reducing to 3.0 near the crust, is made up of rocks containing lighter elements, such as silicon and oxygen. The **crust** is of even lower density because more of the lighter elements are present. The most abundant are silicon, oxygen, aluminium, potassium and sodium. The crust varies in thickness — 5 km beneath the oceans and 30–50 km below continents, but up to 70 km under the highest mountain ranges.

Although the theory of plate tectonics has retained this general threefold division, new ideas have suggested a division of the crust and part of the mantle into the lithosphere and the asthenosphere. The **lithosphere** consists of the crust and the upper mantle, approximately 80 km thick. This is divided into 12 large plates and numerous smaller plates. These are the continental and oceanic plates. The lithosphere is highly resistant to deformation due to its high viscosity or finite strength. The **asthenosphere** lies below the lithosphere for several hundred kilometres. It is much more 'plastic' in consistency; the rocks are softer and more easily deformed.

The theory of plate tectonics is based upon these differences between the deformational properties of the lithosphere and the asthenosphere. The rigidity of the plates means that the stresses occurring where new crust is formed at a ridge (where two plates are moving away from each other) are transmitted to the plates on either side of the ridge. Where two plates are moving towards each other, this energy is usually dissipated without deforming the plates as one plate slips underneath the other. Hot spots around the core generate thermal convection currents in the asthenosphere, which causes magma to rise towards the crust and then spread before cooling and descending. This circulation of magma in the asthenosphere causes the plates to move. The plates of the lithosphere can be viewed as 'floating' on the more dense material of the asthenosphere. This is a continuous process, with new crust being formed along the line of constructive boundaries between plates (where plates are moving away from each other) and older crust being destroyed at destructive boundaries (where plates are moving towards each other). The table below shows some differences between continental and oceanic crust.

Continental crust	Oceanic crust
35–70 km thick	6–10 km thick
Over 1500 million years old	Less than 200 million years old
Density 2.6 (lighter)	Density 3.0 (heavier)
Variety of rocks, mainly granite; silicon, aluminium (SIAL) and oxygen	Mainly basalt; silicon, magnesium (SIMA) and oxygen

Evidence for plate tectonics

Plate tectonics theory revolutionised the study of earth sciences. The theory had its roots in the ideas put forward by earlier workers in this field. As early as the seventeenth century, Francis Bacon had noted the 'jigsaw fit' of the continents; the bulge of eastern South America fitting into the indent of the west African coast. In 1912, Wegener suggested that the continents had originally, about 300 million years ago, been one large supercontinent, Pangaea, which later split up into a northern land mass (Laurentia) and a southern land mass (Gondwanaland). The present continents were formed by further splitting of these land masses.

Different types of evidence have been put forward to support plate tectonics.

Biological evidence
- Fossil remains in India (distinct brachiopods found in beds of limestone) are comparable to those in Australia.
- Fossil remains of an aquatic reptile are found only in a part of Brazil and in southwest Africa. It is argued that these fossils must have been laid down when these continents were joined. It is unlikely that the same reptile could have evolved in both areas or that it could have migrated across the south Atlantic.
- The evolution of plant and animal species has been influenced by the movement of the continents. As the continents have split, each group has evolved different characteristics. The mammals found in Africa, Australia and South America (all originally part of Gondwanaland) are very different.

Geological evidence

- The distribution of glacial deposits and the orientation of striations on large boulders in Brazil and west Africa indicate that the two continents were originally joined. The formation of these deposits cannot be explained in their present environmental locations; they must have formed elsewhere and then moved.
- The geological sequence of igneous and sedimentary rocks in northern Scotland are identical to those found in eastern Canada, indicating that they were laid down under the same conditions in one location.

In the 1950s, there was considerable exploration of the crust. Information came from deep-sea drilling undertaken by the US National Science Foundation and studies of rock magnetism and the age of rocks. When magma cools and solidifies, iron particles are aligned with the prevailing magnetic field. Studies of these 'fossil' magnetic fields in older rocks (palaeomagnetism) reveal that the poles have shifted over time and that the Earth's magnetic field has undergone reversals. Evidence from different continents for this 'polar wandering' did not match and this can only be explained by the assumption that the continents have moved.

Symmetrical patterns of magnetic fields either side of the mid-ocean ridges support the idea of sea floor spreading. As magma wells up along the line of the plate boundary in the mid-Atlantic, it cools to form new crust and a magnetic field is fossilised into the rock structure. As the plates move, these rocks are moved further from the boundary. The observed pattern towards Europe and Africa is mirrored by the pattern towards North America and South America. These crustal blocks are moving apart at a rate of up to 6 cm per year; this supports the idea that plate movement is taking place. The age of rocks increases with distance from the line of the mid-ocean ridge. The newest rocks are in the centre of the Atlantic sea floor and are still being formed; the oldest rocks are nearest to the USA and the Caribbean.

Global pattern of tectonic activity

Constructive (divergent) margins

Plates move apart in areas of divergence, either in oceans to form the mid-ocean ridges or when continental crust fractures to produce rifts. As the plates move apart, the space between them is filled with basaltic lava welling up from below. The zone therefore represents one of the youngest parts of the Earth's surface, with new crust being created. Sea floor spreading to the east and west of the oceanic ridge produces topographical symmetry on the ocean floor on either side of the ridge.

Ocean ridges are the longest continuous uplifted features on the Earth's surface, extending for 60 000 km in total length. They rise up to 3000 m above the ocean floor and are up to 4000 km wide. Their precise form appears to be influenced by the rate at which the plates are separating:

- When the rate is slow (10–50 mm per year, e.g. the mid-Atlantic ridge), the rift at the ridge axis is 30–50 km wide and the rift valley is 3000 m deep, forming inward-facing scarps.
- When the rate is intermediate (50–90 mm per year, e.g. the Galapagos ridge), there is a less marked rift (50–200 m deep) and a smoother outline.

- When the rate is rapid (>90 mm per year, e.g. the east Pacific rise), there is a smooth crest and no rift.

There is also volcanic activity along the ridge as basaltic magma rises along the flanks to form submarine volcanoes which may rise above sea level, for example Surtsey to the south of Iceland. These volcanoes form with sides of low angle (shield volcanoes) because of the low viscosity of basaltic lava, which has its origin in the mantle. Eruptions are frequent but relatively gentle.

As the new crust cools and spreads, transform faults are produced at right angles to the plate boundary. The parts of the spreading plate on either side of these faults may move at different rates, leading to friction between the sub-sections of the plate, which causes earthquakes. These earthquakes are shallow-focus, i.e. they originate in the lithosphere plate near the surface of the Earth.

Continental rifts form where the lithosphere is deformed under stress. This produces large-scale features caused by the downthrow of rock strata between parallel faults. The best-known example is the East African rift valley which extends from Mozambique in the south, through eastern Africa northwards into Jordan — a distance of 5500 km. In some areas, the inward-facing scarps are 600 m above the floor of the valley and there is a series of parallel step faults on the valley side. Volcanic lava escapes within the rift area. The crust underlying many rifts is much thinner than in neighbouring areas, suggesting that tension in the lithosphere is thinning the plate as it starts to split. The line of the East African rift valley is thought to be an emergent plate boundary — the beginning of the formation of a new ocean as eastern Africa splits away from the rest of the continent.

Destructive (convergent) margins

As the crustal plates move towards each other, three different situations can develop:
- oceanic plate moves towards oceanic plate
- oceanic plate moves towards continental plate
- continental plate moves towards continental plate

Different processes take place at these boundaries to produce a range of features. When oceanic lithosphere is forced under other oceanic or continental lithosphere, then the process of subduction occurs. On the margins of the Pacific plate, ocean trenches and volcanic island arcs are formed. These features are produced where the collision between plates takes place well offshore. If the oceanic plate subducts beneath continental plate, then trenches and fold mountains are formed and volcanic activity takes place.

In oceans that are 'closing', i.e. being reduced by subduction, the convergence of the plates takes place below sea level. As the plates converge, the oceanic crust subducts and moves down into the asthenosphere. The sinking lithosphere is much colder than the asthenosphere and it is brittle. As stresses increase, the sudden failure of the lithosphere triggers earthquakes along the line of the subducting plate; these may be shallow-, intermediate- or deep-focus earthquakes. This zone of subduction, of varying angle, is called the Benioff zone. When the upper surface of the sinking lithosphere has reached a depth in the asthenosphere where the temperature is about 1400 °C, the rocks making up the lithosphere begin to soften and melt. Because these are of lower density than the surrounding asthenosphere, as they melt they rise towards the surface as plutons of magma. These produce volcanoes on the surface of the non-subducting plate, fed by material from the subducting lithosphere. The rising magma consists of andesitic lava from the melting plate; it creates complex, composite, explosive volcanoes. This island arc of volcanic activity is aligned in parallel with the line of the plate boundary and the subduction zone. The displacement of the island arc from the line of subduction depends upon the angle of the Benioff zone: the steeper the angle, the closer the island arc to the line of subduction.

As the oceanic plate subducts, it drags down the leading edge of the non-subducting plate to form a trench that is also parallel to the line of subduction. A convergence rate of 30 mm per year appears to be required to produce the whole range of these features.

When oceanic lithosphere collides with continental lithosphere, the more dense oceanic plate (3.0) subducts beneath the less dense (2.6) continental plate. An example of this is where the Nazca plate subducts beneath the South American plate. The down-warping of the margin of the non-subducting continental plate again forms a trench. Sediments that have accumulated on the continental shelf on the margin of the land mass are deformed by folding and faulting. During periods of volcanic activity, intrusion of magma adds to the stresses in the region. These sediments are folded and uplifted by compression and convergence to form fold mountains, as in the case of the Andes along the Pacific coastline of South America.

The subduction process again causes the release of plutons of andesitic magma to produce explosive volcanoes within the fold mountain belt. Earthquakes also occur in this zone.

When the colliding plates both consist of continental crustal lithosphere, the plates have a much lower density than the underlying asthenosphere and this limits the extent of any subduction. The Himalayas were formed by the collision of the Indian and Eurasian plates as they moved towards each other, closing the intervening ocean by subduction. The sediments on the margins and floor of this ocean were folded up in large overfolds to form the Himalayas — up to 350 km wide and extending for 3000 km.

Because there is little subduction, there is no volcanic activity, but the collision point (the suture line) can induce shallow-focus earthquakes.

Conservative (passive) margins

When two crustal plates slide past each other and the movement of the plates is parallel to the plate margin, there is no creation or destruction of crust. This is termed a conservative or passive margin. There is no subduction and therefore no volcanic activity associated with this type of margin. The movement of the plates creates stresses between the edge of the plates. As sections of the plate rub past each other, the release of friction triggers shallow-focus earthquakes. The San Andreas fault in California is along the line of a conservative margin where the Pacific and North American plates move parallel to each other. They are both moving in the same direction but at different speeds. Transform faults run at right angles to the margin.

The map below shows the locations of the main types of plate margin.

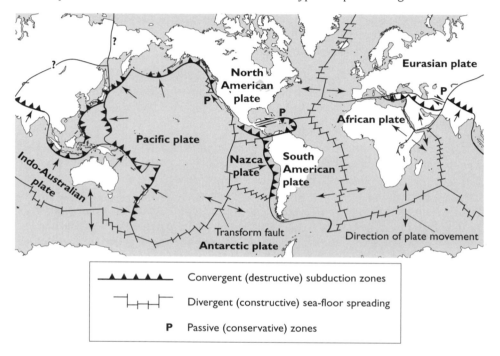

Hot spots

Plume volcanoes are not related to plate margins; they can be found in the interior of plates. They are related to more localised hot spots or plumes in the mantle, above which lava is poured out onto the Earth's surface. The reason for such hot spots is not clear, but they could be caused by a concentration of radioactive elements within the mantle. The plume is the magma source. The hot spots are stationary, so active volcanoes only occur above the hot spot. As the plate moves over the hot spot, a line of volcanoes is created, but only the plume over the hot spot is active; the others are extinct volcanoes. Subsidence of the crust under the weight of each volcano has caused former volcanic islands to sink, to form seamounts. The Hawaiian Islands in the Pacific form a chain, created when the Pacific plate moved slowly northwestward over a hot spot located beneath the present island of Hawaii (the remaining active volcano).

People and the environment

Hazards

Introduction

Hazards have been defined as perceived natural events that threaten life and property but they may also result from human action, such as burglary in urban areas. Remote volcanic or earthquake events that pose no threat to life or property should not be considered as hazard events.

The study of hazards should be made under the following headings:

- **Origin** — the processes that cause the hazard event. For volcanic and earthquake hazards, for example, this involves the geophysical processes that bring them about.
- **Distribution** — the spatial pattern made by the hazard event. Tropical cyclones (or hurricanes) occur only in certain tropical areas; earthquakes and volcanoes are generally associated with tectonic plate boundaries.
- **Frequency** — the occurrence over time of the hazard event. This is not always easy to estimate for some hazards.
- **Effects (or nature)** — the impact of the hazard upon the physical and human environments. Some commentaries differentiate hazard impact on the human environment into, firstly, the effect upon people and, secondly, the impact upon the built environment (buildings, roads and other communication systems, dams, power and water supply systems etc.). With many hazards, it is possible to identify primary and secondary effects.
- **Magnitude/scale** — the size of the impact, or the area over which the hazard event has an effect. There are many methods of measurement: some physical processes have magnitude scales, for example the Richter scale for earthquakes or the Saffir–Simpson scale for hurricanes; some scales incorporate the possible effects upon people, for example the Mercalli scale for earthquakes; other observers use death tolls or the cost of damage through insurance figures. The evidence for scale can therefore be taken from a number of sources, but it is important to understand the reliability of the evidence. The Richter scale may tell you the force of the earthquake, but it does not give you its overall effect upon people and the built environment. Hazard events in MEDCs may cause low loss of life but high damage costs, whereas the reverse is often true in LEDCs.
- **Management** — this covers:
  - prediction. For some hazards, it is possible to give warnings that will enable action to be taken to reduce the impact. Improved monitoring, information and communications technology have meant that predicting hazards and issuing warnings have become more important in recent years.
  - prevention. The ideal situation in management would be to prevent the occurrence of the hazard event. For most hazards this is entirely unrealistic, and the best that can be achieved is some form of modification, often to the environment, through control.

  – protection. This aims to protect people and the built environment from the impact of the hazard, but also covers attempts to modify losses with insurance (particularly in MEDCs) and aid (usually in LEDCs). In MEDCs, areas affected by major hazards are able to draw on central government funds.

- **Response** — this can be made at an individual or collective level. Perception of hazard is influenced by many factors, such as past experience, values, personality and expectations. Response depends upon perception of the hazard and attitudes to it, but also upon the economic ability to take action and the technological ability to carry out that action. The way in which people perceive hazards and the responses that they make can be classified into:

  – fatalism. This is the acceptance that hazards are natural events which are part of everyday life — for some they are 'God's will'. Action is a direct response, usually for safety. Losses are accepted as inevitable and people remain in the area.

  – adaptation. We can prepare for, and therefore survive, the hazard event(s) by prediction, prevention and/or protection, depending upon the economic circumstances of the area in question.

  – fear. The perception of the hazard is such that people feel so vulnerable to the event(s) that they are no longer able to face living in the area and move away to regions perceived to be unaffected by the hazard(s).

- **Evaluation of success** — all attempts at management should be looked at in terms of how successful they have been in prediction, prevention or protection. For example, using dynamite to divert lava flows on Mount Etna, or pouring sea water on lava fronts in Iceland. On the other hand, the Japanese felt they were well-prepared for earthquakes and yet in Kobe (1995) over 100 000 buildings were destroyed and the death toll reached over 6000 (with 35 000 injuries).

Earthquakes

Origin

The causes of earthquakes are covered in the section on plate tectonics (pages 29–34).

Distribution

Most earthquakes are associated with the boundaries between tectonic plates and sometimes with the eruption of volcanoes. Some earthquakes, however, are found on relatively stable continental crust, these usually being associated with the reactivation of old fault lines. It has even been suggested that human activity could have been responsible for a few earthquakes by putting pressure on rocks and fault lines through the weight of water in large reservoirs.

Effects

Some see the primary effect of earthquake as simply ground shaking, followed by the secondary effects of soil liquefaction, landslides, avalanches, tsunamis (tidal waves) and the effects upon people and the built environment. Others view most of the above effects as primary, along with collapsing buildings, destruction of road systems and other forms of communication, and service provision rupturing (gas, water, electricity). Secondary effects are seen to consist of tsunamis, fires (from ruptured gas mains or collapsing electricity transmission systems), flooding, disease, food shortages and disruption of the local economy. Some of the effects on the human environment are short-term; others occur over long periods.

Magnitude/frequency

Earthquakes are measured either on the Richter scale (a ten-point intensity scale) or on the Mercalli scale, which attempts to put the earthquake in the context of the human and built environments. Seismic records enable frequency to be observed, although they date back only to the middle of the nineteenth century.

Management

Earthquake prediction is difficult. Regions at risk can be identified through plate tectonics, but attempts to predict earthquakes a few hours before the event, based upon monitoring groundwater levels, release of radon gas, or even unusual animal behaviour, are questionable. Fault lines such as the San Andreas can be monitored, and changes in the local magnetic field can be measured. Areas can be mapped on the basis of geological information and studies into ground stability, in order to predict the impact and produce a hazard zone map which can be acted upon by local or even national planners.

Prevention is thought by almost all to be impossible, although it has been suggested that fault lines could be encouraged not to 'stick' by some means of lubrication (oil, water) or even explosions!

Protection really means preparing for the event. Buildings can be made more earthquake-resistant with better structures or features, such as rubber shock absorbers, cross bracings and concrete weights that act like a pendulum when the building shakes. (Older buildings/structures can be retro-fitted with devices to make them more earthquake-proof.)

Education is a major factor. This includes instructions on how to prepare for such an occurrence (securing homes, appliances and heavy furniture; getting together 'earthquake kits' etc.). Children can have earthquake 'drills' in school. Some technology can be made available, such as gas pipe cut-offs. First-aid training can be given, as it may be some time before medical services reach the area. The emergency services can be set up to deal with such events (heavy lifting gear, for example), and could be given vital information from monitoring programmes to get them in a state of readiness. People in MEDCs are urged to take out insurance to cover such eventualities. In LEDCs, the provision of aid from both international agencies and developed countries may be needed for immediate relief and for reconstruction of the built environment and redevelopment of the economy — something that can take many years.

Volcanoes

Origin

The causes of vulcanicity are covered in the section on plate tectonics (pages 29–34).

Distribution

Most volcanic activity is found at constructive and destructive tectonic plate boundaries. Volcanic activity is also present in the Hawaiian Islands (Pacific Ocean), which are believed to lie over a hot spot.

Effects

Volcanic hazard effects can also be classed as primary or secondary. Primary effects include lava flows, pyroclastic flows, ash and tephra fall, and volcanic gases. Secondary effects include flooding resulting from melting icecaps and glaciers, lahars (mudflows), volcanic landslides, tsunamis and the impact upon the human and built environments, such as buried and collapsed buildings, destruction of infrastructure, and complete termination of agricultural activities. The ejection of huge amounts of volcanic debris into the atmosphere can reduce temperatures across the planet and is believed to have been an agent in past climatic change.

Magnitude/frequency

There have been attempts to classify volcanic activity by noting the physical differences in eruptions using a table that runs from 0 (non-explosive) to 8 (very large). The impact of volcanic activity is usually measured, as with earthquakes, in terms of loss of life or the cost of damage to the built environment. To determine the frequency of eruption of any volcano, its previous history of eruption can be read by vulcanologists/geologists in the deposits associated with the volcano itself and within the wider region that it can affect.

Management

It is easy to locate volcanoes, but it is very difficult to predict exactly when some volcanic activity will take place. The previous history of the volcano will be important, along with a complex monitoring system. At the present time, research is being conducted to see if it is possible to give a fairly exact time for an eruption, using the shock waves that are produced as magma reaches towards the surface of the volcano, expanding cracks and breaking through other areas of rock. There was some success in predicting the recent eruption of Popacatapetl in Mexico, but it remains to be seen if such techniques can be applied to all volcanoes.

As with earthquakes, protection means preparing for the event. Monitoring the volcano will give a time when the area under threat should be evacuated. This includes observations of land swelling, earthquake activity, changes in groundwater levels and the chemical composition of that water, emission of gases and magnetic fields. Once the lava has started to flow, it is possible, in certain circumstances, to divert it from the built environment by means of digging trenches, controlled explosions or by pouring water on the lava front. In Hawaii, barriers have been built to protect villages from future lava flows and this has also been done in some areas as a protection against lahars. As with earthquakes, some land-use planning has been tried, with high risk areas being avoided. Foreign aid to LEDCs may be required for considerable periods of time as volcanic events can be prolonged. Such aid is needed for monitoring, emergency shelters and food, long-term resettlement of the population and restoration of the economic base.

Tropical cyclones (hurricanes)

Origin

Tropical cyclones are violent storms between 200 and 650 km in diameter. There are several conditions that need to be present in order to generate such a disturbance:

- an oceanic surface temperature of over 26 °C
- a depth of ocean of at least 70 metres
- low-level convergence in the lower atmospheric circulation
- a large enough Coriolis force to generate spin in the system
- rapid outflow of air in the upper troposphere

Distribution

Tropical cyclones occur between latitudes 5° and 20° north or south of the equator (nearer the equator, the Coriolis force is insufficient to generate spin). Once generated, they tend to move westwards to be at their most destructive in the Caribbean Sea/Gulf of Mexico area, the eastern side of central America (east Pacific), the Arabian Sea and Bay of Bengal, off southeast Asia (where they are known as typhoons), off Madagascar (southeast Africa), and northern Australia (where they are known as Willie-Willies).

Effects

Tropical cyclones cause damage in several ways:

- Winds often exceed 150 km per hour and have been known to reach over 300 km per hour. Such winds can bring about the collapse of buildings and severance of electricity and communication networks.
- Heavy rainfall (sometimes 100 mm per day) causes severe flooding and landslides (such as in Hong Kong).
- Storm surges flood low-lying coastal areas and result in salt contamination in coastal agricultural regions.

Magnitude/frequency

Tropical cyclones are measured on the Saffir–Simpson scale (from 1 to 5), which takes into account the central pressure, the wind speed, storm surge and damage potential. As with other natural hazards, magnitude is often measured by death toll or the cost of repairing the damage caused by the event. The average lifespan of a tropical cyclone is 7–14 days. Tropical cyclones in any area occur in distinctive seasons:

- Caribbean/Gulf of Mexico — August–October
- southeast Asia — May–December
- Bay of Bengal — October–November
- northern Australia — January–March

Every year, 70–75 tropical cyclones develop, of which one-third affect southeast Asia (Japan, Taiwan, eastern China and the Philippines). There are 8–10 hurricanes per year in the Caribbean/Gulf of Mexico area.

Management

The prediction of tropical cyclones depends on the state of warning systems. Weather bureaux, such as the National Hurricane Centre in Florida (USA), are able to access data from geostationary satellites and from land- and sea-based recording centres. The USA also maintains a round-the-clock surveillance of tropical storms that have the potential to become hurricanes by the use of weather aircraft. Such information is compared with computer models so that a path can be predicted and people warned in order that evacuation can take place. It is essential that such warnings are correct, as there is a high economic cost associated with an evacuation, and populations may refuse to heed this advice in future.

Like other natural hazards, hurricanes cannot really be prevented, but there has been research into the effect of cloud-seeding to cause more precipitation over selected areas of sea, which would result in a weakening of the cyclonic system.

Protection means being prepared. People are made aware of how to strengthen their homes and commercial properties. Where storm surges are a potential problem, land-use planning can identify the areas at greatest risk and developments can be limited in such localities. Sea walls, breakwaters and flood barriers can be built and houses can be placed on stilts. As with other natural phenomena, people in MEDCs are urged to provide themselves with insurance, whereas in LEDCs it is important that aid is available both in the short term and long term, as the damage to the economic base of the affected area is likely to last for a number of years.

Burglary in urban areas
Origin
The origins of crime are much debated, and are not considered in the specification.

Distribution
There is no doubt that the incidence of burglary tends to be higher in inner-city areas. Insurance premiums are highest for city areas with low-numbered postcodes. The figures for reported burglary offences in the West Midlands in 1999 were 12.4 per 1000 households for the Halesowen/Stourbridge/Lye/Cradeley/Kingswinford division and 36.9 per 1000 households for the Birmingham Central division.

Frequency
Frequency of burglary is difficult to estimate because records are incomplete. Several sources are used to obtain some idea of the problem. These include:

- police records. Not all crimes are reported, for various reasons — fear of retaliation, loss too small to bother about, goods uninsured, willingness to sort it out without recourse to authority (burglar is known to the victim).
- insurance company records. However, some people are not insured. Premiums are often highest in inner-city areas (reflecting risk) and some addresses may find it difficult to obtain insurance.
- British Crime Survey
- the media

In terms of frequency through the year, it has been noted that holiday times (particularly summer) and Christmas are periods when the incidence of burglary rises.

Effects (nature)
The hazard takes several forms:

- removal of goods from property
- damage to property caused when trying to gain entry

- invasion of privacy
- psychological damage — this may be so severe that people almost barricade themselves in their property, or move away from the area

Management

Insurance companies 'predict' crime by area in setting insurance premiums.

It is difficult to separate prevention and protection for this hazard. Trying to prevent the burglar from operating in the first instance must be the priority of any government (this, of course, goes back to 'origins' and the reasons why people commit the crime). Most people try to prevent the burglar gaining access to property with some form of protection. This can be done on several levels. The individual can protect their property by alarms, walls/fences, window locks, security lighting, dogs etc., and by having adequate insurance to cover losses. A collective response can be to establish a Neighbourhood Watch.

At an organisational level, various initiatives have been set up by the police and by local/national governments, including community policing (or simply more police on the beat in targeted areas), CCTV cameras, larger penalties imposed by the courts, and TV and newspaper campaigns. In recent years, the idea of defensible space has come about, where new housing developments have an input from several sources into how the design of property and its layout can deter the burglar by offering no easy entry or quick exit. Such designs are now a feature of many inner-city developments. The great danger with all these initiatives is that although records may show the schemes to be working in one particular area, where burglary has fallen, the overall level of burglary has not fallen, indicating that the crime has simply been displaced from a 'hard' to an 'easy' area.

Organisations such as Victim Support offer help to those affected by crime, such help being both practical (how to deal with insurance companies, emergency repairs, loss of official documents and how to try to obtain compensation) and supportive (counselling and advice).

Transmittable disease

A number of diseases could be studied for this section, including malaria, cholera, typhoid, ebola, lassa fever and even foot-and-mouth disease. Geographers are concerned with many transmittable diseases because they do not spread evenly throughout the world and thus resources to cope with the management of them vary between areas. Understanding the geography of a disease helps to make sense of the social, cultural and economic impact it is likely to have across the world and within different countries.

Acquired immune deficiency syndrome (AIDS)

AIDS is the result of a viral infection brought about by HIV (human immunodeficiency virus). There is much conjecture as to the origins of this virus. Some believe that it is a man-made disease, produced from some chemical weapons laboratory; others think that it spread from the animal population (probably monkeys) to man in Africa.

The disease is spread in several ways:

- exchange of body fluids during sexual intercourse
- sharing needles and syringes in drug abuse
- via contaminated blood transfusions
- from mother to child during pregnancy

Distribution/frequency

There are three main patterns of distribution:

- Pattern 1 — countries that began the spread in the late 1970s, mainly among the homosexual, bisexual and drug-using communities. Heterosexual spread is increasing. This covers North America, Latin America, western Europe and Australia.
- Pattern 2 — countries where the spread has been essentially through heterosexual contact. This covers the bulk of sub-Saharan Africa.
- Pattern 3 — countries where the spread was later (in the 1980s), brought in by travellers and in imported blood for transfusions. This covers eastern Europe (including the former USSR), all of Asia, the Middle East and north Africa.

By 2000, it was estimated that there were over 34 million people worldwide living with HIV or full-blown AIDS, of which 70% were living in the countries of sub-Saharan Africa. North America had 900 000 people with the disease and western Europe 520 000 (1.5% of the world total). It has been estimated that 8.6% of the adult population of sub-Saharan Africa is HIV positive. There are nine countries with 10% or more of the adult population infected. They are: Botswana, Kenya, Malawi, Mozambique, Namibia, Rwanda, South Africa, Zambia and Zimbabwe. South Africa is regarded as having the fastest-growing infection rate.

Evidence for frequency and scale can be obtained from medical records (from doctors and hospitals), national government health department records and the media. However, these figures can never be totally accurate for the following reasons:

- Medical records are confidential to the patient.
- Many people with HIV are not aware that they are infected.
- The social stigma of AIDS means that many sufferers do not report the illness until it is into its late stages.
- AIDS is not always given as the cause of death because the sufferer may have died from another related disease.
- It has been suggested that the disease has been overestimated in Africa in order to obtain money from wealthier governments and charities.

Effects

The United Nations has estimated that nine out of ten sufferers do not know they have the virus in the early days of infection. Most do not die from AIDS itself but from other diseases which they are unable to fight off. Just as important in terms of effects are the attitudes of other people to the disease. Sufferers may experience prejudice in terms of their employment and social life. This may extend to the immediate family; there have been cases where children have been ostracised because one of their parents had the disease.

In Africa, the effects on families have included loss of income-earning opportunities, the diversion of effort and income into care and medicine, and withdrawal of children from school. There has been a huge effect on farming, with AIDS threatening food-growing and income-earning potential in areas already facing food shortages. Some countries have been faced with large numbers of orphans as a result of AIDS, which has placed pressure on local resources.

Management
By plotting the course of an outbreak, it may be possible to predict the future spread and to identify areas where resources should be concentrated. With AIDS, the first stage would be to try to prevent the disease totally by seeking a vaccine. Research can also be directed towards alleviating symptoms through the use of anti-retroviral drug treatments, thereby extending the lifespan of those with the virus.

Many countries hope to prevent the spread of the disease through education and advertising campaigns, particularly by targeting vulnerable groups such as homosexuals and intravenous drug users. Raising the profile of the disease in schools through sex education has been a major feature in the UK. Other campaigns in the UK have included free needles for drug users, free condoms, blood screening and warnings to tourists about their behaviour in foreign countries.

Looking after people with the disease and their families has become the responsibility of many agencies. Several charities are involved in the UK, including the Terrence Higgins Trust and London Lighthouse.

Urban multi-hazard environments
The features of hazards that affect the urban environment are similar to those already studied (origin, frequency, evidence, effects and management), but here you should also examine:
- interrelationships between hazards
- types of response by people living in the area

The example of Los Angeles (California)
Los Angeles is affected by many hazards (or potential hazards). In the physical environment there are earthquakes and tsunamis, heavy rainfall and river flooding, coastal flooding, drought, fires, mudslides and landslides, and smog (some texts refer to this as 'modified physical'). In the human environment there are burglaries and other crimes, gang warfare, racial violence and AIDS. There may be others!

Interrelationships
Some hazards of the urban environment are linked: one hazard may contribute to another. There are various forms of relationship, for example:
- a simple, direct relationship (e.g. earthquakes ⟶ landslides; drought ⟶ fires; earthquakes ⟶ crime; earthquakes ⟶ tsunamis; heavy rainfall ⟶ mudslides)
- where one particular hazard can contribute to many other hazards

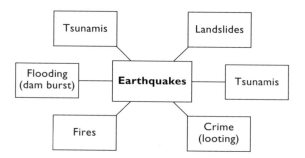

- a more complex linear relationship (e.g. drought ⟶ fires ⟶ flooding — fires remove vegetation, thereby decreasing interception)

Interrelationships may exist through a central factor. In Los Angeles, over the last 40–50 years, there has been massive urban sprawl. This may have been a factor in several hazards, such as:

- river flooding — as the city has sprawled, more and more land has gone under concrete and tarmac, particularly in the surrounding hills. Less infiltration leads to more surface runoff.
- fire — the low-density urban sprawl has left vast areas of shrubland between housing developments. Fire is therefore a greater risk.
- smog — the vast area of the city has encouraged widespread car usage and has discouraged a city-wide public transport system. Car exhaust fumes have been the major factor in the decline of air quality in the Los Angeles basin.
- the spread of the city has led to extremely affluent suburbs (e.g. Beverly Hills and Bel Air), which are White-dominated, and impoverished inner areas (e.g. Watts), dominated by Afro-American and Latin American communities. There is evidence of great division between such areas. The 1992 Rodney King affair (White police/Afro-American suspect) led to widespread rioting and looting in some parts of the city.

Responses

There are three main ways in which the people of Los Angeles tend to respond to living in a multi-hazard environment:

- Some accept the fact that the hazards exist but are not prepared to do much about it — 'it won't happen to me' syndrome.
- Some recognise the hazards and do something to protect themselves, for example take out insurance, fit burglar alarms, prepare for earthquakes (e.g. gas cut-offs, drills, education) or move house to be above smog areas. Such people tend to be affluent enough to afford precautions and they expect the authorities to act by insisting on smog control, earthquake-proof buildings, emergency services, flood control etc. They are also willing to pay the increased taxes that result from implementing such measures.
- Living in such a multi-hazard environment may become too much of a strain, forcing some people to move away. This often happens after a major hazard event,

such as the Northridge earthquake of January 1994, and the riots and looting in 1992 which followed the acquittal of the policemen in the Rodney King affair.

Competition and conflict over the use of a resource at a local scale

This is best examined with reference to a real conflict that is taking place or has taken place in your local area. This allows you to investigate the issue as it develops through time, and to seek the opinions of people from both sides of the argument. Clearly, if the issue is local to you, as well as being local in scale, then you will have greater access to the issue as it progresses.

There have been a number of conflicts at a local scale that have achieved more public notoriety. These include the Newbury bypass, the second runway at Manchester Airport, and the new container terminal in the Southampton area. Each of these would also be suitable for study using national media sources of information.

Such conflicts are resolved by either market processes or planning processes, or in some cases a combination of these. **Market processes** operate in an environment where the ability to pay the going rate takes precedence over any local or national concerns. Often, objectors cannot afford to outbid the developer. Consequently, the latter gets its way, and the development goes ahead with the minimum of consultation. Consultation often takes the form of an opportunity to voice objections or propose counter-proposals, but with no right of independent arbitration or appeal.

Planning processes attempt to provide a means by which local authority planners:
- listen to the local community (and therefore appear to be more democratic)
- listen to the organisation responsible for a proposal of change
- have overall development control

Any refusal by a local authority planning committee may lead to an appeal, or may result in the developer going to a higher body, for example national government in the form of the Department for the Environment, Food and Rural Affairs. Planning processes are costly (in terms of both time and money) for local authorities.

Planning committees may:
- require or negotiate modifications to be made to offset the opposition
- request additional provision of facilities (such as better road access), which the authority might have to provide if the development goes ahead and which may placate some of the local opposition

Therefore, planning committees need to weigh up:
- the gains from the proposal against its negative aspects
- the conflicts between differing groups within a local community
- the wider benefits that may accrue from a local scheme against the local opposition

An example of conflict over the use of a resource at a local scale

The conflict

The western bypass of Newbury — a conflict over the use of land.

The proposal

To build a new bypass to the west of Newbury to ease north/south-moving traffic through the town along the A34 (which also forms part of the Euroroute EO5).

The participants

These include:

- the local council of Newbury
- the local residents of Newbury
- the farmers of the area to the west of Newbury
- the road hauliers who wish to travel through Newbury from the north/M4 to Southampton
- the Department of Transport and the Highways Agency
- Friends of the Earth
- the 'Third Battle of Newbury' group
- the Newbury Bypass Supporters group

The problem

Most of the A34 consists of dual carriageway, except for the section through and to the south of Newbury. Here there are four roundabouts, which have to deal with 50 000 vehicles a day, 15% of which are heavy goods vehicles. Traffic congestion is severe for large parts of the day and, in the summer, often through the night as tourist traffic adds to the volume. Traffic also travels to and from the M4 which lies 3 miles to the north of the town, so there are links to south Wales.

The processes used to resolve the problem

Planning processes meant planners could:

- listen to the local community, and to objectors to the proposal
- listen to the organisation responsible for the proposal of change, and the reasons for it
- have overall development control in the context of the wider public benefit

The proposal to build the bypass went to appeal, and a Public Enquiry was held in Newbury under the chairmanship of a judge. Alternative views on the need for a bypass, together with alternative views on the route of the bypass, were heard. After a lengthy and costly enquiry, the decision to construct the bypass was upheld, and construction began in 1998. The bypass was opened in 2000.

Attitudes to the issue

- The 'Third Battle of Newbury' group was against the proposal because the road would cut through several Sites of Special Scientific Interest, destroy archaeological sites, damage the site of the First Battle of Newbury (1643) and increase the risk of flooding where bridging structures would constrict the flow of rivers.

- Newbury Council was for the route of the bypass as it would reduce traffic through the centre of Newbury by 36%, cutting goods vehicles by 88%. Only three houses along its 9.5 mile length would have to be demolished, and public transport policies would have a greater chance of success.

Human geography

Transnational corporations and the global economy

A transnational corporation (TNC) is a business organisation that operates in at least two countries. In particular, it is a means of coordinating between one centre of strategic decision-making and production in at least two countries. The organisation tends to be hierarchical; often the headquarters and Research and Design (R&D) are in the home country (country of origin) with branch production plants overseas. Examples of TNCs include IBM, Sony, Philips, Ford, Nissan and Nestlé.

Nissan produces approximately 2.6 million vehicles annually (2001) at its 20 vehicle manufacturing plants in 16 countries around the world. These include seven Japanese plants, four of which are engaged in vehicle production; the others build engines and other major components. Overseas manufacturing facilities are located in the USA, the UK, Spain, Mexico, Taiwan and other markets. The European R&D centre has been developed at Nissan UK (Washington, near Sunderland).

An indication of the extent to which an organisation is transnational is the relative proportion of its operation that is based outside the home country. UNCTAD's index of transnationality is calculated as the average of the ratios of foreign assets/total assets, foreign sales/total sales and foreign employment/total employment. On this basis, Nestlé, with its home base in Switzerland, has an index of 94, i.e. 94% of its operation is based outside its home country.

The geographical significance of TNCs is based upon three key factors:
- TNCs can control or coordinate economic activities in different countries and develop trade within and between units of the same corporation in different countries. In this way, the TNC has control over terms of trade and can reduce the effects of quota restrictions on the movement of goods.
- TNCs have the ability to take advantage of spatial differences in factors of production and government policies at the global scale. They can exploit differences in the availability of capital, labour costs, and land and building costs; they can take advantage of cheaper labour in less developed economies. For example, in 2002, Dyson, the household cleaner manufacturer, announced plans to relocate from its production plant in Wiltshire, UK to Malaysia to take advantage of much lower labour rates. TNCs can also take advantage of different government policies — tax levels, subsidies/grants, environmental controls (less strict in some countries) — and can get round trade barriers by locating in the market economy.

- TNCs have geographical flexibility and can shift resources and production between locations at the global scale to maximise profits.

TNCs therefore have a very important role in linking economies at different scales — global, regional (within a continental area), national and local.

Nissan was attracted to a location within the European Union because of quota restrictions on the import of Japanese vehicles. By producing vehicles within Europe, they could be considered as European and gain entry to the large EU market. Their success has been followed by Toyota (near Burnaston to the southwest of Derby) and Honda (Swindon), where 2500 workers produce over 150 000 cars annually. Honda production is aimed particularly at the European market, together with some export to the Middle East and Africa.

Although TNCs are active in almost all economic sectors, they are especially important in certain activities, including:
- resource extraction, particularly for geographically localised materials such as oil and gas
- manufacturing, for example:
  - technologically advanced industries (computers, scientific instruments, pharmaceuticals, microelectronics)
  - large-volume consumer goods (cars, tyres, televisions, electrical goods)
  - mass-produced consumer goods (branded goods, cigarettes, drinks, breakfast cereals, cosmetics)
- services, such as banking/finance, advertising, freight, hotels and fast-food operations

The major advantage of their large size and scale of operation is that they can achieve economies of scale, allowing them to reduce costs, finance new investment and compete in world markets. These firms serve a **global market**; they have therefore globalised manufacturing. US firms began this trend, with Ford setting up its first European plant in Manchester in 1911. Overseas investment is dominated by US companies. Many European firms began to invest overseas after the Second World War, while Japanese firms have become significant in the global economy since the mid-1970s. Large firms have a wider choice when locating a new plant, although governments may try to influence locational decisions in order to protect home markets.

TNCs can either supply foreign markets through world trade or opt for direct investment overseas to serve the immediate market.

Direct investment results in location decisions at two scales:
- choice between countries. This often reflects political considerations. Governments are keen to attract companies because inward investment creates jobs and boosts exports which assist the trade balance. Because of their influence, TNCs have the power to trade off one country against another to achieve the best deal.
- location within a country. TNCs have the financial resources to research several

sites in order to take advantage of communications, access to labour, low cost of land and building, and government subsidies.

Globalisation of production can be achieved in three main ways:

- host market production. Each manufacturing unit produces a range of goods and serves the local national market. Plant size is limited by the size of the national market.
- product specialisation for a global market. Each plant produces only one product for sale throughout a regional market consisting of several countries.
- transnational integration. Each plant performs a separate part of the process. Linkage takes place across national boundaries in a chain sequence (vertical linkage) or components are moved to a final assembly plant in one country (horizontal linkage).

Social and economic impacts of TNCs on their host countries and country of origin

Inward investment by TNCs can have significant positive effects upon social and economic developments within the host country, at both a national scale and a local/regional scale. In 2000/01 the UK attracted 869 projects from foreign firms, creating over 71000 jobs. Although this may be considered a relatively small number of jobs compared with total employment of over 20 million, a large proportion of the investment for these projects came from outside the UK; they were not financed by the Exchequer using contributions from taxpayers, although some of these firms will have been attracted by the incentive of government subsidies. At a local or regional scale within the host country, the injection of new investment can trigger the multiplier effect through the operation of the process of cumulative causation.

A major factor encouraging industrial concentration is **external economies of scale** or **agglomeration economies**. These advantages arise from outside the firm itself, unlike internal economies of scale that result from the large-scale operation of the production plant. External economies can be divided into two components:

- **localisation economies**. These occur when firms linked by purchase of materials and finished goods locate close together. This reduces transport costs between supplier and customer, leads to faster delivery times (which in the case of TNCs may enable just-in-time operations) and allows better communication, facilitating greater personal contact between firms (which is important for TNCs in monitoring and maintaining quality).
- **urbanisation economies**. Cost savings may result from an urban location allowing linkages between manufacturing and services. Industries depend upon functions such as auditing, advertising and cleaning. Although large companies can provide some of these for themselves, they often find it cheaper to contract out the work to specialist firms. Savings also result from the economic and social infrastructure of the area that is already established before the arrival of the new firm.

The location of a TNC in an area may increase jobs through industrial linkage; firms that supply components to the new plant will increase their business and may add to their workforce; firms that distribute products also experience growth through linkage. However, some domestic firms in direct competition with the new company may lose business and employees. The arrival of the TNC will also stimulate the local economy, perhaps reducing local unemployment, increasing disposable incomes in the area and creating additional demand for housing, transport and services. This creates an upward spiral in economic terms. To safeguard domestic firms, governments negotiate a local content element of the final product; consequently, the TNC agrees to work towards an agreed percentage of components being supplied from the host country.

As well as creating employment, many TNCs introduce new methods of working in their plant and in their supplier companies. This is brought about through the operation of quality management systems which monitor the standard of output in supplier firms, and through the initiation of just-in-time (JIT) component supply. Total quality or zero defect is an essential part of this philosophy. Therefore, a company's standards are monitored in order to meet the demands of the TNC. In this way, TNCs are influential in modifying working practices and the transfer of technology to firms in the host country.

If the TNC has located in an LEDC, this could lead to increased urbanisation, greater opportunities for female employment through the introduction of low-skilled manufacturing jobs, and a declining or ageing population in rural areas as young people seek opportunities in the urban areas. TNCs may also bring unwelcome environmental changes: increased air and water pollution, loss of land given over to the building of the plant and houses, and loss of habitat for wildlife.

The impact of TNCs on their country of origin is largely negative in an economic sense. If a firm takes its production overseas, then this is likely to result in increased unemployment, both in the plant and in linked component suppliers, and a reduction in disposable income. A downward spiral will be created, and the multiplier will operate in reverse. (Dyson's move to Malaysia will remove at least 800 jobs from its current location in Wiltshire.) However, individuals and institutions that are share-holders in the TNC will reap higher dividends if the firm makes a greater profit as a result of locating overseas.

Newly industrialising countries as hosts and countries of origin of TNCs

The last 20 years have seen increases in the level of industrialisation in several developing countries. These have been described as newly industrialising countries (NICs). The main areas of rapid manufacturing growth have been east and southeast Asia (South Korea, Hong Kong, Taiwan), southern Asia (India) and Latin America (Brazil, Mexico, Argentina). The rapid expansion of investment by TNCs is one of the major reasons for their growth.

The key attractions of NICs as hosts of TNCs are cheaper labour costs, cheaper land costs and weaker environmental and planning laws. In addition, NICs provide access to an expanding domestic market for consumer goods, while locating in an NIC reduces the effect of tariff barriers, and many raw materials are available locally.

The ability of TNCs to take advantage of these location factors has been influenced by rapid developments in communication and transport technology. It is now much easier to control production in an NIC from a remote headquarters in a developed economy. The use of container transport and bulk carriers has reduced the cost of transport over large distances. Costs of transporting key personnel, raw materials, components and products have also been reduced as a proportion of total cost. Satellite communication, telecommunications and the growth of the internet have enabled rapid transfer of information and management control.

Malaysia has attracted a number of industrial concerns in the last 20 years. On the Bayan Lepas Industrial Park (Penang) major companies such as Hewlett Packard (4000 workers) and Bosch (3500 workers) have established plants. Major corporations such as Microsoft and IBM have been attracted by government incentives to locate south of Kuala Lumpur on a development that the government visualises as an Asian version of Silicon Valley. In Taiwan, the Hsinchu Science Park, 70 km southwest of the capital city Taipei, provides a number of incentives to investors: freedom from import duties on machinery, raw materials and partly processed goods (components); freedom from commodity or business tax on goods exported; provision of up to 49% of paid-up capital in approved joint ventures with the government; and grants for R&D developments.

NICs have also emerged as countries of origin of TNCs. Although the general tendency is for such TNCs to locate production plants in surrounding LEDCs, where wage rates and land costs are even lower than in the NIC, some companies have located in the MEDCs. LG (Lucky Goldstar) located in south Wales to take advantage of UK government incentives and wage levels that are lower than those in South Korea.

The emphasis is usually on low-technology, labour-intensive products — often those not produced in the developed world. TNCs from NICs are usually small; most are involved with petroleum refining and mineral extraction. Goldstar, Samsung and Hyundai are South Korean TNCs, producing machinery, electronics and vehicles respectively. They have developed into TNCs as a result of the development of managerial and research skills fostered by the location of TNCs from developed countries in the NICs. The increased availability of capital from entrepreneurs and governments and a rise in wage levels have encouraged these firms to relocate in cheaper areas. New markets are emerging in LEDCs as they begin to develop; a number of companies have moved into China to satisfy this potentially huge market. These new TNCs from NICs are simply following the pattern established by companies from the economically more developed world.

South Korea has risen to tenth place in world economies with 27% of labour employed in manufacturing. Of the top 25 countries in world manufacturing production, only Brazil, Mexico, Taiwan, Argentina and South Korea are considered to be NICs. These account for 75% of manufacturing production in all developing countries, but this represents only about 6% of world manufactured goods, compared with the USA producing 24% and Japan, 14%.

Attitudes to TNCs

Positive attitudes

- National governments favour the investment, job creation and increased revenue, although existing industry may be threatened.
- Component firms may enjoy opportunities to supply the incoming TNC.
- Construction firms benefit from investment and jobs in building plant/supporting infrastructure/new housing.
- Transport firms and energy supply companies enjoy increased revenue/jobs.
- The newly employed benefit from increased income and living standards, while there are new opportunities for female workers.
- Providers of local services/shopkeepers etc. experience increased trade from a rise in local disposable income.
- Farmers are presented with a larger market for their produce.
- Trade unions welcome the additional jobs but may fear a loss of influence if the new firm adopts a single-union approach.

Negative attitudes

- Local councils (city councils) experience increased pressure on services.
- The unemployed may face an increased social gap between those in work and those not.
- Local residents experience increased road traffic and loss of greenfield sites, though some may have gained employment.
- Environmentalists' views will depend upon the type of manufacturing, but they are likely to object if development will result in any form of increased pollution, or loss of habitat or right of way.
- Competing firms face loss of sales as a result of the TNC locating in the home market. They may resent foreign firms receiving subsidies, grants or incentives that are not available to domestic manufacturers.

International migration and multicultural societies

International migration

International migration involves the movement of people across national boundaries. Migration may be:

- voluntary or involuntary (forced)
- temporary or permanent
- legal or illegal
- of varying scale, characterised by the volume of movement and the distance involved
- motivated by economic, social, political, cultural or environmental factors
- selective on the basis of age, gender, educational level, or a mass movement involving all groups within the population

In many cases, there is a distance–decay element to migration, in which the number of migrants declines as the distance between the origin of the migrant and the destination increases.

Economic moves are often of relatively longer distances, whereas many refugee movements are short-distance moves from neighbouring countries. Other factors that distort this general relationship include:

- economic differences — differing levels of gross domestic product (GDP) promote movement
- colonial links — movements from former colonial territories to the mother country
- family links — movement to reunite family members
- political regime — encouraging movement to a more democratic society
- government policies and immigration controls — recruitment of labour or assisted passages (as in the case of Australia, which attracted population from the UK in the post-war period)

Major forms of international migration

Economic

There are three key areas of movement between LEDCs of the developing south and MEDCs of the affluent north. In the 1980s, a total of 3.5 million migrants entered the USA from Mexico; of these, 700 000 were legal migrants, 2.3 million were amnestied or legalised, i.e. they were granted legal status once in the USA, and about 500 000 were illegal migrants. This desire to enter the USA is clearly triggered by differences in GDP and the opportunity for casual employment within the farming communities in the south and southwest. There is also movement across the north–south divide from north Africa into Europe, particularly into southern France and Italy, where the long coastline is vulnerable to illegal entry of migrants. Much of the migration into France reflects links with colonial territories, for example Algeria. Many migrants have moved to join relatives who migrated in an earlier phase. In Asia, there is movement into the richer economies of Japan and Hong Kong from Malaysia and the Philippines.

Movement also occurs from LEDC to LEDC, for example from Pakistan and Bangladesh into the Middle East for work in the oil and construction industries. Many of these movements are temporary, for the duration of the work permits.

In a similar way, there has been movement between MEDCs for temporary work, such as UK construction workers to other parts of the EU (Germany), but also over greater distance, for example between the UK and the USA. Despite its concerns over immigration from LEDCs, the US government has been enthusiastic in its encouragement of highly qualified/skilled workers (e.g. scientists, doctors and nurses) from other countries. This highly selective migration is referred to as a brain drain.

Refugee movement

In 1951, the United Nations defined a refugee as:

> someone who, owing to a fear of being persecuted for reason of race, religion, or membership of a particular social or political group, is outside the country of his/her nationality and is unable or, owing to such fear, is unwilling to return to that country.

Now, those fleeing civil wars, ethnic/tribal/religious violence and environmental disasters such as earthquakes and famine are also regarded as refugees.

In March 2002, the UN High Commissioner for Refugees (UNHCR) estimated that there were some 22 million people of refugee status in the world. Many of these were large-volume, non-selective, short-distance moves into neighbouring countries. Such moves are generally temporary, with migrants returning after the cause of the migration has ended. Recent examples of refugee movement include:

- over 2 million from Ethiopia, Sudan and Somalia, primarily due to famine
- over 6 million from Mozambique as a result of war, degradation of land and natural disasters (flooding)
- over 1 million Kurds fleeing from oppression in northern Iraq
- 100 000 Tamils seeking to escape oppression in Sri Lanka
- 7000 of the 11 000 residents of Monserrat evacuating the island after the first recorded volcanic eruption of the Soufriere Hills in July 1995 (Monserrat is a British Territory, so the migrants were resettled in the UK)

Changing forms of international migration

The main changes in international migration over the last 30 years include:

- a decrease in legal, life-long, economic migration, particularly from LEDCs to MEDCs. The reception areas have provided less opportunity, with increased legislation and fixed quotas for immigration, and more careful monitoring/checking at points of entry. Deindustrialisation has reduced the number of low-skilled jobs available. Many LEDCs, as source regions, have seen a growth of opportunities for employment as TNCs have exploited raw materials and established branch plants to take advantage of lower production costs.
- an increase in movement between MEDCs, for example in EU countries where restrictions have been removed to allow free movement of labour. The Schengen Agreement has allowed movement across borders without passport control. However, there has been less movement between the UK and the USA, where work permits are difficult to obtain for the less highly skilled.
- an increase in attempted illegal, economically motivated migration (for example Mexico to USA, and north Africa to Europe). Tighter border controls and entry requirements have made it more difficult to enter legally.
- an increase in short-term migration. Countries are increasingly placing time limits on work permits, while temporary refugees are being resettled.
- increased movement between LEDCs. The scale of this movement fluctuates according to the varying political and environmental/ecological conditions.
- a decline in social migration since many families have now been reunited. However, some moves from LEDCs to MEDCs still tend to be for this purpose rather than new migration.

Multicultural societies

A multicultural society is one that contains members from a wide variety of national, linguistic, religious or cultural backgrounds. It is often an emotive issue, particularly when cultural differences are interpreted as racial differences. Although many modern-day groups are thought to have descended from three broad racial types — negroid, caucasoid and mongoloid — the distinctions are now so blurred that race has little scientific relevance. Although skin colour remains a visible distinguishing feature, people differ in terms of their ethnic background — language, religion and culture. Multicultural societies are the product of migration, but also may be the stimulus for migration as persecuted groups seek to escape oppression. Groups within a multicultural society may be integrated to a greater or lesser degree. The operation of apartheid in South Africa illustrates a lack of integration, while Singapore and Brazil represent more tolerant attitudes among various groups.

South Africa's difficulties lay in the fact that, until 1990, the Black population (which makes up about 76% of the total population) was politically, economically and socially dominated by the White population (about 13% of the total). The country's policy of apartheid (which means living apart, or separate development) was further complicated by the presence of 4 million Coloureds (of mixed descent) and 1 million Asians. The White population, a mixture of Dutch settlers (Afrikaners or Boers) and British and German settlers, viewed themselves as first-class citizens; Coloureds and Asians enjoyed some rights, but were seen as second-class; Blacks had virtually no rights outside their homelands, the areas where they were forced to live. Since 1990, the recognition of the African National Congress and the release of Nelson Mandela and other political prisoners, has led to post-apartheid developments within South Africa.

Singapore represents a more tolerant attitude between the dominant Chinese (76%), Malays and Indians (22%) and the minority Europeans and Eurasians. Brazil also has very little racial prejudice, even though its census recognises a number of divisions: Whites (lighter skin), Mulatto (darker skin with an element of European descent), Blacks (pure African descent), Orientals (more recent migrants from south/southeast Asia) and Amerindians (indigenous native population). These examples illustrate that multicultural societies can be harmonious.

In MEDCs, the issues tend to reflect the extent to which the host country encourages and welcomes the opportunity for cultural diversity, or attempts to minimise the differences in cultures. Early migrants were often a source of cheap labour, working in low-paid construction, transport or health service jobs. Low incomes led to concentrations of ethnic groups in the inner city areas of the major cities. These concentrations have been reinforced by later migrants seeking the support and security of living near friends or relatives within an ethnic community. This has reduced the opportunity for assimilation or integration in terms of housing, and ghettos may develop in these areas.

Language differences can also be an issue. Migrants find it difficult to obtain employment and integrate if they do not speak the host country language. Second-generation migrant children, educated in the host country, do speak the language and have different aspirations from their parents. They are more likely to integrate, and this can cause tension within the ethnic groups as they are seen to adopt the culture of the host country.

Migrants are likely to follow a different religion from the host population. This may cause friction with employers and authorities as the migrants wish to adhere to their own religious calendars and practices.

Educational opportunities may be more restricted for migrants. Language differences and prejudice can result in problems for children who tend to be in poorer, lower-achieving schools. Local authorities may have to fund extra provision in terms of specialist language teaching; this additional expenditure is viewed by some as an issue.

Attitudes to international migration and multicultural societies

Migration is often welcomed during periods of economic growth when there is a labour shortage; the host population does not want to do low-paid, unskilled work. But resentment often occurs during periods of recession when migrants are seen as taking jobs. This has occurred in the cases of migrant workers in Germany, France and the UK.

Large-volume movement of refugees places a high cost on the host country. LEDC hosts cannot afford to support a large influx of migrants and lack the finance for temporary housing or shelter. The governments support the humanitarian response but need help from the UN, other countries or relief organisations in order to fulfil this role. In an MEDC such as the UK, the recent increase in the number of asylum seekers has required the construction of specialist accommodation to house people while their applications for asylum are being processed.

Many countries are tightening their rules on immigration and the allocation of work permits and entry requirements. This makes it more difficult for both economic refugees and for genuine asylum seekers to gain entry. There has been growing pressure to restrict immigration in Europe. The greater ease of movement within the EU has led to stronger external controls. There are some concerns that Europe's traditional role as a place of sanctuary for refugees is being replaced by hostility, with 'Fortress Europe' repelling migrants.

Governments have taken some positive steps to address these issues. In the UK, there has been legislation to combat discrimination: anti-racism laws, employment laws and equal opportunity acts. Although children have been encouraged to integrate in schools, there has also been freedom to develop Muslim and Jewish schools within the community.

In theory, the decrease in the number of permanent migrants should reduce pressure on housing, but those of the second generation do not want to remain trapped in low-cost, inner-city areas. They resent the racism they experience when they try to move to other areas. The second-generation migrant population has greater social and economic aspirations. The language differences become less obvious as migrant populations become established and this allows for increased integration in some areas. Some urban areas display considerable harmony and integration of ethnic groups with a high profile in the local community, through representation on local councils or as elected MPs. In other areas, there is tension and intolerance. Issues tend to be highlighted by factors other than increased number of migrants; resentment and racism increase during periods of higher unemployment.

The issues are less pronounced in LEDCs. State benefits/support are not usually provided and housing schemes tend to be more integrated. This results in migrants being less obviously segregated into specific parts of urban areas, and there is greater social tolerance.

Separatist pressures and the grouping of nations

There are currently two apparently contradictory processes operating within Europe. In some countries, regions are seeking to break away from the control of centralised government; there are signs of fragmentation, with separatist pressures threatening to break up national areas into smaller units. On the other hand, many national units are strengthening economic and political links between each other; they are integrating and moving towards greater centralisation of power.

Separatist pressure

Separatist pressure is an attempt by a group of people within one or more countries to achieve greater autonomy (ideally, independence) from a central government from which they feel alienated in some way. Such groups often have a different language, culture or religion from the rest of the state and are geographically peripheral within that area. They may feel that they are geographically remote from the centralised government and that they do not receive adequate support, particularly with regard to economic development and growth.

Reasons for separatist pressure include:
- minority language or culture within a larger political area
- an area of economic recession compared with the wealthier core of the country
- minority religious grouping
- perception that exploitation of local resources by national government produces little economic gain for the region
- collapse of a socialist state
- peripheral location to the political/economic core

In Canada, the French-speaking Quebecois seek independence from the rest of Canada. In the UK, the Scottish Nationalist and Plaid Cymru campaign for an independent Scotland and Wales respectively, has been partly satisfied by the establishment of the Scottish Parliament and the Welsh Assembly and some devolution of decision-making powers. The Scottish National Party feels that the exploitation of North Sea oil and gas has done little to develop the economy of Scotland, which is remote from the seat of government in London.

The collapse of Communism in eastern Europe created a wave of nationalism, particularly in Yugoslavia and the former Soviet Union, which led to subdivision and the creation of new states, for example Croatia, Slovenia, the Czech Republic, Slovakia and Moldova.

Social groups often feel alienated or insignificant in an increasingly complex industrial society. This feeling is increased further if the region is remote or peripheral, in which case it may seek a sense of community based on local culture and tradition. The strengthening of the EU has led many nationalist groups to think that they would have a better chance of developing economically if they were independent.

Spain has a number of communities with strong nationalist movements based primarily upon language differences. Distinctive languages are found in the regions of Galicia (Galician), Catalonia (Catalan) and the Basque country (Euskara). Euskara is unique and distinctive. The extent of the Basque country is subject to debate: there are four provinces in northern Spain that reflect Basque culture — Vizcaya, Guipuzcoa, Alava and Navarre — together with Labourd, Basse-Navarre and Soule in southwest France. Franco, who was to lead Spain until 1975, executed or imprisoned thousands of Basque nationalists. The use of Euskara on buildings/road signs or in publications was banned and the teaching of the language was declared illegal. The culture and language was suppressed for over 40 years. In 1959, a nationalist political organisation, ETA (Euskadi ta Askatasuna), was formed; in the 1960s it declared war on the Spanish state. It operates a violent campaign targeting police, security forces and political and government figures and buildings. It has stated that its armed struggle will continue until it has achieved an independent Basque country comprising both the Spanish and the French provinces. In 1979, a government-held referendum resulted in massive support for autonomy of the Basques and a Basque parliament was created. ETA continues its violent campaign to create an enlarged Basque territory including the French provinces.

The grouping of nations

Since the Treaty of Rome was signed in 1957 to create the European Economic Community (EEC), comprising six countries, nine other states have joined the now titled European Union (EU):

- 1957 — initial membership of France, West Germany, Italy, Belgium, Netherlands, Luxembourg
- 1973 — UK, Ireland, Denmark
- 1981 — Greece
- 1986 — Spain, Portugal
- 1995 — Austria, Finland, Sweden

The initial treaty was signed only 12 years after the end of the Second World War. Although the treaty was established to develop closer union between member states, and it had a very clear economic emphasis, it was considered important to tie West Germany into an economic union as a guarantee for future peace. The dominant purpose of the EEC was to promote peace within Europe by encouraging prosperity and greater international cooperation.

The aim of the EU is to promote the economic integration of the member states by:

- reducing tariffs and barriers to trade between members
- establishing a common external tariff for imports from outside the EU
- allowing free movement of labour, capital and other factors of production
- establishing common policies on agriculture, fishing, industry, energy and transport

If countries develop greater interdependence and their economies become more integrated, then their economies will benefit and the standard of living in those countries will improve. Trade encourages competition and this promotes greater efficiency through the operation of economies of scale. Each producer has access to a much larger market. The expansion of the EU to 15 members has created a potential market of some 377 million people (2002). However, less efficient producers are forced out of business and this encourages countries to specialise in those goods that can be produced most efficiently. This develops comparative advantage for production.

For most of its existence, the EU has operated as a **customs union** in which internal trade barriers are removed; the union is protected by common external barriers. The creation of the Single Market in 1993 created a **common market**, which allows free movement of products and people.

Negotiations on the creation of an **economic union** began in 1991 at Maastricht. The main aim of this treaty is further to strengthen economic and political links between members. This would significantly reduce the control national governments have over their own economies and policies. This has been very controversial in all EU countries. However, despite the complexity of the treaty and the lengthy negotiations, by the end of 1993 all EU countries had ratified the treaty, although the UK and Denmark have negotiated a number of opt-out clauses. The move towards full economic and monetary union was implemented in 2002 with the adoption of the Euro throughout most of the EU.

Attitudes to political changes

Attitudes towards EU membership vary within and between countries, although there is overwhelming evidence that many other national units would like to join this powerful trading bloc. Post-Communist governments in eastern Europe are seeking to develop economic and political links with the EU. It is likely that the EU will increase in membership over the next decade. Attitudes are mixed.

Arguments in favour include:
- increased trade opportunities with reduced tariff barriers
- ease of movement for workers between member countries
- ease of movement for travellers — the removal of passport/customs checks
- greater support for agriculture
- support for declining industrial regions, including urban regeneration
- protection against cheap imports
- wider transport and environmental policies
- a common currency — preventing currency fluctuations and simplifying transactions
- reduction in the risk of war between member countries

Reasons against include:
- an increased feeling of centralised government — *in* Europe, but *not run by* Europe
- a loss of sovereignty — key decisions are taken in Brussels or Strasbourg by what some regard as an undemocratic bureaucracy

- loss of financial controls
- perceived remoteness of EU institutions
- increased paperwork for receiving funds (e.g. set-aside for farmers)
- a quota system which affects national industries (e.g. fishing)
- pressure to adopt EU legislation and uniformity (e.g. the Social Chapter/minimum wage, Bosman ruling on soccer transfers, the Euro banana/sausage etc.)
- difficulty in meeting requirements and costs of EU directives (for example pollution emissions)

Whatever views individuals may hold, it is likely that the EU will strengthen its role further within the world economy.

Development issues within an LEDC or MEDC (excluding the UK)

The core–periphery relationship

Friedmann produced a model of the economic development of a country, with particular reference to the changing economic relationships within that country. The model progresses through four stages of development:

- Stage 1 — a number of relatively independent local centres, each of which serves a small region, with no settlement hierarchy.
- Stage 2 — the development of a single strong **core** during the initial phases of industrialisation, with an underdeveloped **periphery** in the remainder of the country. Economic development occurs in the core region which has a specific advantage over the rest of the country, for example a natural resource or dense population. The initial advantage is maintained by cumulative causation as more capital, entrepreneurs and labour move to the core.
- Stage 3 — the **core–periphery** structure becomes transformed into a multi-nuclear structure with the national core and a number of peripheral sub-cores. These may develop due to large regional markets or important natural resources.
- Stage 4 — a functional interdependent system of cities, resulting in national integration and maximum growth potential.

Four types of area can be designated from this model:

- the **core region** — the focus of the national market and seedbed of new industry and innovations. It has a concentration of economic development.
- upward transitional areas — regions with some form of natural endowment, characterised by inward migration of people and investment
- the **periphery** or downward transitional areas — regions with unfavourable locations and resource bases, characterised by outward migration of people and investment. Unemployment is high and living standards are low.
- **resource-frontiers** — areas where new resources are discovered and exploited

Case study — China

The People's Republic of China is the world's most populous country (1.26 billion) and the second largest economy, measured on a purchasing power parity basis (after the

USA). In 1978, the Chinese leadership began moving the economy from a centrally planned economy to a more market-orientated system. The system operates within a political framework of strict Communist control, but with an increasing influence of non-state managers and enterprises. The authorities have increased the decision-making powers of local officials and plant managers in industry, permitted a wide variety of small-scale enterprise in services and light manufacturing (such as electrical goods and small machines), and opened the economy to increased foreign trade and investment.

In the mid-1990s, these ideas were taken a stage further with the creation of special economic zones (SEZs) and open cities. These are areas of the country that are allowed to attract foreign companies to set up factories there. Foreign investors receive preferable tax, tariff and investment treatment. This also means that foreign companies now have access to Chinese markets, in areas where wages and production costs are particularly low. China benefits from this arrangement by earning money from abroad and increasing the skills of its workforce. Both SEZs and open cities were initially concentrated on the east coast, facing the Pacific and Taiwan. For example, in the vicinity of Hong Kong four SEZs — Zhuhai, Shenzhen, Shantou and Xiamen — were established, in addition to the acquisition of the commercial hub of Hong Kong itself. Open cities also stretched down this coast from Tianjin in the north to Shanghai to Zhanjiang in the south. There are now over 2000 SEZs, heavily concentrated along the Pacific coast. This area is rapidly developing into the economic **core** of the country.

In 1991, China authorised some foreign banks to open branches in Shanghai and allowed foreign investors to purchase shares in Chinese stocks. In 2001, over $41 billion were received as foreign direct investment (FDI), the main sources being the USA, Japan, Taiwan and TNC investment through Hong Kong.

FDI has taken place not only on the Pacific coast, but also in key locations within the body of the country. Perhaps one of the most contentious aspects of this concerns the Three Gorges Dam on the Yangtze River. The main aims of the project are:

- to control flooding and reduce the incidence of associated death and destruction
- to generate hydroelectric power (HEP) — it is hoped that the scheme could generate 18% of the country's present energy needs
- to provide water for irrigation for more cash crop production (cereals and flowers)
- to improve river transport by eradicating the large numbers of rapids on that section of the river

Other **resource frontiers** exist where there is potential for mineral development, particularly fuels. They include:

- the major oilfields at Daqing and Liaohe in northeastern China, which produce two-thirds of the country's oil
- offshore oilfields on the east coast in the Bohai Sea (east of Tianjin), the Pearl River mouth and the Gulf of Tonkin
- gas fields to the west, in Xinjiang Province

Questions
&
Answers

This section contains questions based on Module 4. There are two types of question: structured and essay. Each question is worth 25 marks. You should allow 45 minutes when attempting to answer a question; the time on the structured questions should be divided according to the mark allocation for each part.

The candidate responses are attempted under strict examination conditions. These demonstrate thorough knowledge, a good understanding and a sound technique on the essay questions. However, in most cases, there is some room for improvement.

Examiner's comments

Candidate responses are followed by examiner's comments, indicated by the icon 🄮. These point out areas for improvement and common errors, such as lack of clarity, weak or non-existent development and misinterpretation of part of the question.

For structured questions, examiners use a system for each section involving 'levels'. For this unit, the sections in the structured questions are marked using only two levels:

- Level I answers generally contain simple material such as lists of activities, the nature of a hazard, definitions/descriptions/links expressed in only a few words, recognition of attitudes, lists of advantages/disadvantages, straightforward statements etc.
- Level II answers generally contain detail, and in some cases an attempt to classify material. If asked for, a discussion is entered into, rather than simple descriptive material being presented. Comparisons of attitudes and responses are made. Good use is made of exemplars/case study material.

The answers to all the essay questions are marked using an assessment grid, based on the bullet points given in the question. Examples of such assessment grids are provided for Questions 8 and 9. Note that the grids contain up to 20 marks for the geographical content (G) and up to 5 marks for skills, including quality of language and level of exemplification (S). Unlike the structured questions, some aspects of the grid run to four levels but not all aspects of the question are considered beyond Level III. Level IV is awarded for well balanced discussions that are wide-ranging in their coverage, answers that develop links clearly between process and outcome, and responses that show a consistent breadth *and* depth across the bullet points. Answers to essay questions that reach Level IV can expect to receive marks from 21 up to the maximum.

Geopolitics: integration and separation

(a) Describe the spatial expansion of the European Union (EU) over the last 30 years. (5 marks)

(b) Discuss the reasons why countries have joined, and continue to want to join, the EU. (7 marks)

(c) Many groups express concern that over the last 30 years, political power within the EU has become increasingly centralised. Describe two pieces of evidence they would use to support their view. (5 marks)

(d) Within many countries, there are separatist movements demanding greater autonomy from the central government. With the aid of examples, discuss the possible consequences within a country of pressures for separatism. (8 marks)

Total: 25 marks

■ ■ ■

Candidate's answer to Question 1

(a) Following the grouping of the six Common Market countries — France, Germany, Belgium, the Netherlands, Luxembourg and Italy — in 1957, there have been three main stages of expansion. In 1973, the UK, Ireland and Denmark joined. In 1981–86, the Mediterranean enlargement took place when Spain, Portugal and Greece joined, which completed the natural limits of the EU on the southern side. The most recent expansion took place in 1995 — the EU was enlarged from 12 to 15 countries when Sweden, Finland and Austria joined.

 The candidate shows knowledge of the EU expansion in terms of countries, but does not indicate how the Union expanded in a spatial manner, except for the point regarding the southern area. A better answer would have made more reference to the central core in northwest Europe and moves to incorporate countries in this region. The most recent expansion can be seen as a beginning of a movement eastwards. Nevertheless, this receives credit for the reasonably accurate list of countries as they have joined the EU plus the Mediterranean spatial material, and is awarded a Level II mark of 3 or 4 out of the 5 available. Questions such as this are set to a 30-year time limit, but as the beginnings of the EU go back to the 1950s, the examiner would allow the opening material as 'scene setting'. If you are looking at expansion or change, you have to start somewhere.

(b) The reasons for countries wanting to join the EU vary, but are mainly political and economic. The original grouping of six countries appeared to occur for economic reasons. The abolition of tariffs and customs barriers between the six countries led to great economic growth and prosperity between 1957 and 1973. Each country, however, also had political motives for joining. Germany saw the Union as a way of reconciliation with France following the Second World War. France saw the Union as an opportunity to gain a greater degree of control over the powerful German coal industry, which it saw as a threat to its own. The Benelux countries wanted greater political integration in Europe, as did Italy, which was geographically isolated.

The UK and Ireland joined largely because they saw that it would hinder their economies if they did not. This was a particularly important motive in 1973 as the oil crisis was at its peak at this time. They were also conscious of the fact that they could easily become isolated from mainland Europe. The Mediterranean enlargement occurred for economic reasons, as these countries were less developed and thought the EU would help the development of their economies.

The motive behind the enlargement from 12 to 15 was mainly political, as these countries did not want to become isolated. Their economies were already well developed, so this was not the most important factor. Throughout the growth of the EU, there was the motive of the need to create a large unit that could compete economically and politically with the USA.

🖉 This is a good answer. The candidate initially informs the examiner that the reasons can be placed into categories, in this case political and economic, and makes some reference to the economic growth and prosperity of the period from the late 1950s through to the 1970s. Rather than presenting a generalised answer that would have been credited at Level I in the mark scheme, the candidate attributes particular motives to specific countries such as Germany, France, the UK and Ireland, and makes some attempt to explain the Mediterranean enlargement. The danger with this method is that it can lead to repetition, as several examples could be covered by the same reason. The candidate has given detailed references here, although there are points that could have done with more information, such as the reference to the UK and Ireland, where a little more detail on 'would hinder their economies if they did not' would have helped, as would some reference to how the Mediterranean economies could have developed. The answer also makes repeated references to 'becoming isolated', without really explaining the phrase. Overall, this answer achieves a high Level II mark of 6 out of 7 marks.

(c) The EU's rigid bureaucratic law on the enforcement of the beef ban is evidence for centralisation. The EU set this ban, having not investigated the problems fully. The EU, in this matter, had lost touch with the public. Its decision was enforced and none of the member countries had the ability or the power to address the matter. This top–down decision making, with implementation over all its members, is stark evidence for centralisation.

The establishment of the single currency, the Euro, is another piece of evidence. This has meant a loss of sovereignty among the member states that are now using this single currency. The running of economic, political and social aspects in one currency means that the EU is now acting as one state, with centralised operations.

🖉 This is a good answer. The candidate gives the two pieces of evidence required and shows how these support the view that the EU is becoming centralised. This deserves full marks.

(d) Within a country, separatist pressures create a great deal of nationalist feeling. In the last 30 years, this has been evident in Wales and Scotland, which have been under increased pressure to have a greater degree of autonomy. In Wales, this increased nationalist feeling has led to a revival of the national language. This had been in decline and English had taken over as the main language in the country. Over the last 30 years, Welsh has become more important; it is taught in schools from a very young age and much of the day-to-day business in some parts of the country is now conducted in Welsh. Scotland, too, has demanded greater recognition for its individual culture. An example of this occurred in 1997, when Scottish television companies refused to show English commercials and insisted that they were remade using Scottish actors. Separatist pressures in Scotland have led to different education and legal systems from those in the rest of the UK. There have also been differences in priorities in local government spending.

Separatist pressures can cause unrest, and ultimately result in a greater degree of autonomy being granted to that area. This will have significant political and social effects as these areas now have their own capital to fund certain policies instead of relying entirely on capital from the central government. An example of this is the abolition of university tuition fees in Scotland, which have been retained for students in other parts of the UK.

This is another good answer. For Level II credit, the examiner is looking for material that is detailed and uses relevant exemplar material. As the question also asks for a discussion, good answers are those that try to place the consequences in the context of the country as a whole. This answer is good in both respects, although the candidate could have explored other avenues, such as the emergence of nationalist political parties, civil disobedience and even terrorism. Reference could also have been made to outcomes such as independence or the establishment of local assemblies/parliaments. The only real weakness in the answer is an unwillingness in some parts to include detail, for example relating to 'differences in local government spending' which should have been tied to the material at the end on student financing. With the amount of detail contained elsewhere and a willingness to enter discussion, this answer is placed towards the higher end of Level II, for 6 or 7 marks out of 8.

Transnational corporations and the global economy

(a) With the aid of examples, describe how the growth of global products is linked to the development of transnational corporations (TNCs). (6 marks)

(b) Give *two* pieces of evidence that would show the influence of a transnational corporation on the economy of a host country. Explain how *one* of them would demonstrate that influence. (5 marks)

(c) Describe and suggest reasons for the different attitudes within newly industrialising countries (NICs) to transnational corporations and the investment that they bring. (8 marks)

(d) With the aid of examples, discuss the statement: 'The growth of transnational corporations has been mainly a disadvantage to their countries of origin.' (6 marks)

Total: 25 marks

■ ■ ■

Candidate's answer to Question 2

(a) A global product is a product that is available in a number of countries, for example Coca-Cola. There is a similar approach to advertising in each country and common features of the product, such as taste. The product is marketed under one logo. The growth of global products is linked to the development of TNCs due to the cost of transport of these products. To reduce transport costs, it is easier to produce the final goods at the end destination. A good example of this is Ford in the UK. Although it has parts coming from all over the world, such as engines from Germany, the product is finally assembled in the UK, thus reducing the cost of transporting the car to its UK market.

Another reason why global products have helped to develop TNCs is the need for country-specific features, such as right-hand drive cars for the UK. Also, perishable goods are not easily transported, so they must have manufacturing locations at the end destination (e.g. McDonald's).

Global products have encouraged TNCs to grow owing to trade barriers, such as those set by the EU. It is cheaper to locate in the final destination in order to produce goods there, as protectionist trade blocs will then not apply to the corporation.

e The definition of a global product is rambling, but the candidate is not required within the wording of the question to define the term. The answer, however, is full of material that links global products to TNCs: assembly of components; adaptations to fit local markets; perishable products; and protectionist barriers. There is also good use of exemplar material, although McDonald's is not the best example in this case as it is a service industry. A Big Mac, a product of McDonald's, could be used, however, as an example of a global product. As the links between global products and TNCs are well established in this answer, it is certainly placed towards the top of Level II; with only 6 marks available for the question, maximum credit is awarded.

(b) Two pieces of evidence that show the influence of TNCs on the economy are GNP growth rate and employment statistics in the host country. The presence of TNCs in a host country such as South Korea has the effect of raising GNP in that country. In South Korea, GNP was raised by 88% in 2 years, suggesting that TNCs have had a beneficial effect on the economy. This is also true for other host countries, such as some in Latin America which have experienced growth rates of 12% per annum.

> ✒ The candidate has named two pieces of evidence, as asked for in the question — one the examiner could accept and another which is debatable in this context. Rising GNP is evidence, but 'employment statistics' could mean anything — falling, rising, static? A much better statement would have been **rising formal employment**. 'Employment statistics' would have been correct if the question had asked for 'sources of evidence'. The second part of the question is somewhat better — exemplar material on South Korea is used, although the statistics seem a little exaggerated. However, the candidate still fails to show *how* GNP demonstrates the influence of TNC involvement and, as a consequence, the answer is only of Level I quality, gaining just 2 out of 5 marks. To qualify for marks within Level II, the candidate should have explained how TNCs *raise* GNP.

(c) NICs are countries that have experienced rapid economic industrialisation over a short period of time. An example of this is South Korea. Attitudes towards the effects of TNCs are either positive or negative, and the effects are economic, social or environmental. Evidence from GNP records suggests that TNCs have a beneficial effect on the economy (e.g. South Korea's GNP rose by 88% in 2 years).

There are many positive attitudes towards this from governments, which encourage TNCs to locate in the area (e.g. enterprise schemes such as that in Sunderland, UK).

The unemployed will also have a positive attitude towards TNC investment as many jobs are created. In Latin America, employment has risen by 127% since 1975, as new jobs have been brought to the area. These jobs, however, are not welcomed by all, as TNCs help to change the structural division of labour. Rural–urban migration increases, which often leads to stagnation in rural areas, meaning that there are negative attitudes to TNCs from those who are left. Also, the jobs provided have been mainly for women, which results in positive attitudes by women's rights campaigners, although the male population does not see it that way, especially if they lose their status as the family provider. Thus, the economic advantage of creating jobs has the social disadvantage of conflict among the sexes as the changing role of women develops.

Economically, there is also concern among some governments and economists over their countries' dependence on foreign economies, particularly the dollar. If the US dollar collapses, so will the host's economy, which was the case in the collapse of the Asian Tigers in the 1990s. Despite the great economic and industrial development, there are worrying social effects. A major concern is the exploitation of women in the host countries. There is evidence that companies such as Nike have been forcing long hours, few breaks and harsh working conditions on workers, which has angered many human rights activists.

Another disadvantage is job insecurity: TNCs relocate into cheaper countries, such as China from South Korea, as conditions become more economically favourable elsewhere. Despite this, there are signs that TNCs have improved the standard of living of their workers by providing education to operate machinery. Due to this basic education, there is a positive attitude from both the government and those being educated. Also, there is some evidence that the standard of living improves with better infrastructure and sanitation. In Latin America, provision of fresh water increased from 45% of households in 1975 to 90% in 1990. Thus, there is a positive attitude from locals who have been provided with this water.

Environmentalists, however, have a negative attitude towards TNC growth, as it has resulted in pollution, an example of which is increased air pollution in South Korea and in the major urbanised cities of India.

> There is a lot of information here about the impact of TNCs that could have gone into answering several different questions. What the examiner is looking for is attitudes to TNC involvement and an explanation of those attitudes, not a list of the advantages and disadvantages of TNCs. In other words, the information in this answer has not been well marshalled in order to take the maximum advantage from it. This is one of the most common complaints from examiners on questions of this type. The best way to give a good answer is to identify groups, organisations and people with positive and negative attitudes, and even try to identify where there could be conflicting attitudes (e.g. governments could see the advantageous points along with the negative). The candidate does try to refer to attitudes that might be held, although this is not always put in an exact manner in terms that could be marked at the very top of Level II (8 marks). It is also a great pity that some of the exemplar material is very weak — since the question is about NICs, it is disturbing to find that the first example is Sunderland! The candidate is keen too on Latin America, which is not an example of an NIC! At this level, candidates should be able to identify individual countries; far too many still think that Africa is an example! Given that the candidate has tried some form of classification and that there are a number of recognisable attitudes given, this is marked at Level II, gaining 6 or 7 marks out of 8.

(d) There are both advantages and disadvantages of TNCs in relation to the countries of origin. A major disadvantage is the decline of heavy to medium industries. A good example of this is the textile industry in Lancashire. This was a thriving industry and important to the local economy, but the production has now relocated, due to the growth of TNCs, to cheaper areas of the world, such as India. This decline in manufacturing is due to the spatial organisation of the TNC, which means that although the company HQ and R&D are located in the country of origin, manufacturing moves abroad due to cheaper labour, government grants and less strict environmental laws. Therefore, heavy to medium industry declines in the country of origin.

Linked to this is the decline of traditional industrial areas. As manufacturing is now not the main priority in these countries, areas such as the northwest of England have declined, whereas areas important for R&D, such as the Cambridge Science Park, have expanded. There has also been a decline in male employment as the new, highly skilled jobs often go to females, compared with heavy industry, which is male-dominated.

In contrast, there are advantages to the country of origin, such as growth of employment in areas such as the finance sector and the highly paid jobs in management and research. For this reason, TNCs have forged strong links with universities in the country of origin, for example Cambridge, and they are able to provide jobs for graduates.

There are three detailed Level II points within this answer which are worth 5 of the 6 marks available. They are the loss of traditional medium/heavy industries, the decline of traditional industrial areas with expansion in other places, and growth of employment in service sectors. The point regarding female employment is not well put; it would have been better linked to the service sector rather than to skilled manufacturing. The candidate is assessed at Level II for the point on industrial decline, although the example of the textile industry is not totally correct. The growth of textile industries in countries such as India is not thought to be mainly down to TNC involvement. The candidate refers to both advantages and disadvantages, although the quotation covers only the latter. As the question asks the candidate to discuss the statement, it is legitimate to show how it is not a disadvantage and this material can be credited. The highest marks would go to those candidates who attempted to show whether the growth of TNCs had been a disadvantage or not.

International migration and the multicultural society

(a) Give *two* pieces of evidence that could be used to identify a multicultural society. Suggest how *one* of these pieces of evidence would demonstrate the presence of such a society in an area. (5 marks)

(b) Suggest some of the reasons for the international migrations that have led to the development of multicultural societies in the last 30 years. (7 marks)

(c) Discuss how the forms and levels of international migration are changing. (7 marks)

(d) 'As multicultural societies become more established, there are fewer issues to be addressed.' Discuss the extent to which you agree with this statement. (6 marks)

Total: 25 marks

■ ■ ■

Candidate's answer to Question 3

(a) One piece of evidence is the percentage of ethnic minorities as part of the population, both at a national level and regionally, for example in major cities and conurbations. Another piece of evidence is the presence of foreign restaurants, bars, places of worship and exclusive social clubs. This piece of evidence would indicate that there are cultures/races present in an area that are distinct from the indigenous population. This is a particularly useful indicator, as these places are clear signs that many cultures exist in an area. People from the Indian subcontinent bring mosques and restaurants, for example the Curry Mile in Rusholme, Manchester. West Indians bring carnivals, markets and Pentecostal churches. The Chinese have chip shops and restaurants, such as those in Chinatown in Manchester.

The first sentence is a somewhat obvious statement, but as the candidate qualifies it with some detail, it is just about acceptable. The second piece of evidence, however, probably qualifies as more than one point. The answer then goes on to show how this second piece can be used, which takes the answer up to 4 out of 5 marks. To reach full marks, a little more would need to be said on how such features serve the immigrant community and thereby indicate its presence. It is always a good idea in this context to use exact examples, such as those indicated in Manchester.

(b) When we talk about multicultural societies, we refer to the condition of most developed nations today. Britain, the USA, Germany and other Western societies have experienced much immigration in the past. As a result of these immigrants settling in communities, their cultures are clearly demonstrated in the host country.

One major reason for international migration was the catastrophic effect of the Second World War. The European imperial powers were exhausted economically and in terms of infrastructure. A good example is Germany, with the 'Gastarbeiter'. These were the Turks who flocked to cities to work in car manufacturing and in the construction and transport industries. By the 1980s, the Turks accounted for 3% of the German workforce. The above reason also resulted in migration from old colonies into England and France. Both countries shared problems of a weak economy and a manufacturing industry lacking available labour. The British government opened the way in the 1950s for West Indians to reside and work in the UK. The Caribbean was a former part of the Empire and the Commonwealth. Later, Nigerians and Indians, who were highly skilled but did not have job opportunities in developing countries, used the Commonwealth connection to emigrate in the 1970s and 1980s. Algerians moving to France is a further example.

Another reason is forced migration. This includes the Asian east Africans who were expelled by Idi Amin and used their rights as Commonwealth citizens to move to Great Britain. More recently, there was the forced migration of expatriates from Zimbabwe, whose land was seized. The general trend of all this migration was from poorer to developed nations.

e There are some good points made here, backed up by detailed and appropriate examples. Unfortunately, the candidate has not kept to the last 30 years, making reference in one place to 'the 1950s'. Examiners tend to be generally relaxed about an exact interpretation of the time period, as many migrations of the period began well before the 1970s, but to base a large part of the answer on West Indian migrations into Britain and 'Gastarbeiter' in Germany seems to be missing the point of the question. Many of the general points, however, are correct, and this is awarded a Level II mark of 5 or 6 out of 7. Other points that could have been made include civil wars, famines and natural disasters.

(c) International migration, as epitomised by the 'Gastarbeiter', has declined from what it once was. This is because many of the developed nations have initiated much stronger immigration laws. Great Britain passed the Commonwealth Act in 1962 and a similar law, tough on immigration, in 1968. In the 1980s, the Germans decided enough was enough and offered cash incentives for the Turks to return to Turkey. They also stopped any more foreign workers from being employed by German companies. The French targeted Algerians, offering 10 000 francs or more to encourage them to return to Algeria, as well as tightening immigration laws. This has meant a shift away from voluntary migration from LEDCs to MEDCs.

Now the major form of migration is based on refugee movements, where people are forced to move. Examples are numerous and really started with the plight of the Palestinians in the 1970s after the Middle East War. More recently, there have been the million Tutsi who fled from the Hutus in Rwanda. Ethiopia, because of the great famine in the 1980s, saw mass migration to neighbouring countries. The collapse of communism, signalled by the destruction of the Berlin Wall in 1989, has meant a movement of refugees from eastern to western Europe. Together with others moving from war-torn countries, a common term now applied to such people is that of 'asylum seekers', something which every government is trying to control.

With increasing ease of transport and economic globalisation, many people are going to other countries to set up businesses, and managers are sent abroad by their TNC employers on expansion of the company.

> 🖉 This is a good answer, with plenty of case study material appropriate to the question. The answer does ramble, and could have looked at movements that are definitely on the increase, such as those between LEDCs and between the countries of the EU, rather than from LEDCs to MEDCs. The examiner would also expect to see references to illegal migration, which is becoming a feature of the pattern into developed countries such as the USA, the UK, Germany, France and Italy. However, what has been written is very much to the point of the question and as the candidate has been prepared to discuss, rather than simply describe, the situation, the answer is awarded the maximum 7 marks.

(d) The longer a multicultural society exists, the more likely it is that the migrant population can assimilate and become accepted. The indigenous population becomes accustomed to different cultures and religions; White people are often seen eating in foreign restaurants and putting aside prejudices.

Significantly, the original migrants bring up a second generation which often has far more in common with the indigenous population than their parents do. This means that they are simply accepted as, say, 'British' or 'German' rather than constantly being labelled as foreigners. Once established, the migrants may well improve their situation by working hard and obtaining enough income to move out of the cheaper inner-city accommodation and into the suburbs. Thus, with their economic power they are able to gain a stake in society. Gradually, as they reside longer, they settle in and learn the language and are soon used to the host society. Many organisations will notice that there are a growing number of cultures and will accept them and avoid racist policies. As the old generation, which was used to one culture, is replaced by a younger population that has grown up with other cultures, the attitude within the country will change dramatically.

There are, however, cases that show that no matter how long a multicultural society exists, ignorance will still remain. West Indians have lived in Britain since the 1950s, yet the Brixton and Toxteth riots of the early 1980s and the ensuing reports indicate that racial tension and squalid conditions were still common. Even with long establishment, many are unable to move from the poorer inner-city areas and are caught in a poverty cycle of no skills, lack of education, poor housing, low self-esteem and crime. Many ethnic areas in Britain had, until recently, been suspicious of the police. There was often a mutual feeling from the police towards those ethnic minorities.

The aftermath of the racist murder of Stephen Lawrence, as recently as the 1990s, proves the above point. As a result, many institutions were branded institutionally racist. It seems, therefore, that ignorance continues to pervade the indigenous population long after a multicultural society is established. The problem of inner-city deprivation continues not only in Britain, but also in the 'ghettos' of major American cities. The issue of segregation is always present, as ethnic minorities do not easily assimilate.

This is an excellent answer. The candidate has been prepared to discuss this statement by trying to see both the positive and negative sides of the issue. Too many answers of this type are buried in vague generalities, but that is not the case here. The answer contains very clear, named details. For example, instead of simply stating that racism continues to exist, the candidate has quoted the Stephen Lawrence case and used it well to illustrate the point. Under examination conditions, this deserves full marks.

Plate tectonics

(a) (i) Using *only* a labelled diagram, show the main physical features of a rift valley. *(5 marks)*

(ii) Explain how the processes at work within and below the Earth's crust are responsible for the features that you have shown on your diagram. *(6 marks)*

(b) Describe the characteristics of the fold mountain areas of the world. *(7 marks)*

(c) Discuss how the formation of fold mountains is linked to the processes operating at plate margins. *(7 marks)*

Total: 25 marks

■ ■ ■

Candidate's answer to Question 4

(a) (i)

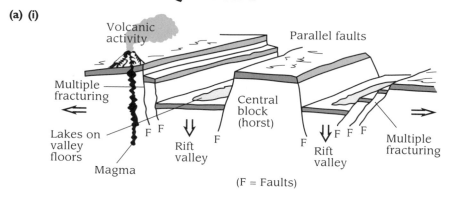

ℓ This diagram is awarded all 5 marks. The points worth credit are: parallel faults; multiple fracturing; dropped sections of crust, often associated with a central block left standing (horst); large lakes along valley floors; associated volcanic activity; and arrows indicating earth movements.

(ii) Rising convection currents bring magma closer to the surface, where it causes crustal upwarping and lateral tension. When the tension is great enough, the crust cracks (rifts) and magma can rise up to fill the gaps. Once exposed, it cools quickly and solidifies, pushing the plates apart and creating a central rift valley between the cracks (faults).

New volcanic material is continually rising up these cracks and pushing the plates further apart. This is occurring in several places under the ocean — the East Pacific Rise in the Indian Ocean and, most notably, along the Mid-Atlantic Ridge. There is also the land-based example of the Great African Rift Valley which stretches over 4000 km from Mozambique in the south to the Red Sea in the north. The rising magma in this case has created many volcanoes in eastern Africa, such as Mount Kenya and Mount Kilimanjaro.

The tension is often so great that instead of one simple crack appearing, the edges of the valley are marked by multiple, and often complex, fractures. On the Mid-Atlantic Ridge, the American and Eurasian plates are moving apart and new land has been produced through volcanic action, such as the island of Surtsey, off Iceland. There is often lateral motion here which produces trans-form faults that run at right angles to the plate boundary.

🖉 This is an excellent answer and it is difficult to see how a better one could have been produced under exam conditions. The material clearly explains how rift valleys are formed and uses plenty of examples. The candidate also distinguishes between those under the sea and those found on land. Although not all the features described in the answer are to be found on the diagram in part (i), the answer receives full credit. Candidates often include a diagram in questions of this type, but there was no need here as this had already been completed.

(b) Fold mountains are characteristically ancient areas and form the highest land on the continent. The composition of fold mountains is generally granite and associated rocks, although regional metamorphism may have occurred to alter some of the original rock types. There is also much sedimentary rock in such mountain areas, often containing fossils, which proves that these areas were once beneath the sea. There is often an extreme contrast between valleys and mountains due to the folding and faulting of the rock. Fold mountains are usually found running in chains, often parallel to each other and on the edge of the continental plate, such as the Andes in South America.

🖉 There is a lot in this answer about the geology of such areas, which is acceptable in the context of the question, but there is not a lot about their appearance, which is also part of their characteristics (it is a geography question!). Points that could be included are: permanent snow cover; ice/glaciers; frost-shattered; rugged/steep; and often associated with volcanic activity, for example the Andes. Also, if there is an observation that they are the highest point on the continent, why not give an example, such as Mount Everest? One point that would certainly qualify at Level II is the classification of fold mountains into young and old. To be awarded these marks, examples need to be added, such as the Alps (young) and the Appalachians (old). The answer presented here is certainly within Level II of the mark scheme, and is awarded at least 5 marks of the 7 available.

(c) Fold mountains can occur at destructive margins. There are two types — subduction zones, which produce Andean-type fold mountains, and collision zones, such as that along the Himalayas.

Subduction zones — the diagram below represents the Nazca plate and the South American plate producing the Andes. Here, the two plates are moving towards each other. The oceanic plate is more dense (3) than the continental plate (2.5), so the oceanic plate is subducted beneath the continental plate. As it sinks, it remelts and then rises up the mantle as it is now lighter. This forms igneous intrusions (batholiths) and also volcanoes, which become part of the fold mountain range. Sea-floor sediments that are scraped up as the oceanic crust sinks are folded and raised up into mountains, along with an island arc which is pushed onto the shore after formation. The area between these two is lifted to form a plateau containing salt water lakes, for example Lake Titicaca. The volcanoes of the Andes are very explosive and produce acidic andesitic lava.

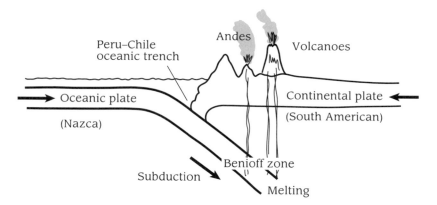

Collision zones — the diagram below represents the Indo-Australian plate moving towards the Eurasian plate, forming the Himalayas.

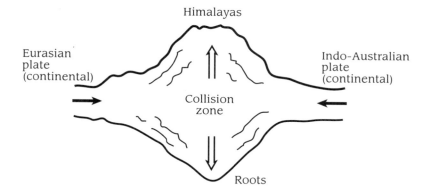

Here, two continental plates meet each other and, as they are of the same density, neither is subducted. Instead, the sea-floor sediments that were laid down between the plates are crumpled upwards to form huge fold mountains. As the plates continue to move towards each other, the sediments are buckled even higher; today the Himalayas are still rising. Many of the rocks in the highest areas of the mountains contain fossils of sea creatures, indicating that the rocks of the Himalayas were formed under the sea.

 This a good answer, covering all the major points that could be expected, and is awarded the maximum 7 marks. There are some slight errors in the text, none of which would reduce the overall mark, though. For example, the candidate is correct in stating that subduction zones are found at destructive margins, but collision zones form their own category as nothing is being destroyed there. There is also some confusion as to how the sediments came to form the Andes. However, the answer is good in its use of exemplar material. It is far better in questions of this type to use an example to show how a process works, since examiners give credit beyond Level I for such material. When dealing with the Andes, the candidate covers vulcanicity in the first place and then goes on to show how the sediments formed into fold mountains. Many candidates fall into the trap of considering only the volcanic activity. Unfortunately, a major textbook tells them that this is so: 'These volcanoes are likely to form a long chain of fold mountains (for example the Andes)'. How a line of volcanoes can be described as a chain of fold mountains is difficult to see! Candidates are well advised to look for folded sediments as well. The use of diagrams is a good idea, although these will not be double-marked, i.e. credit will not be given for text and for the same idea/feature on a diagram. Most examiners mark the text first, and then see whether the diagrams can add anything to that credit. If diagrams are asked for in the wording of the question, then marks will have been set aside for these.

Question 5

Soil profile characteristics

'The characteristics of soil profiles vary because of differences in the parent material, climate, topography, vegetation cover and the amount of time the soil has had to develop. Human activity is another factor that can influence the characteristics of the soil.'

Discuss this statement with reference to *either* podzols *or* brown earth soils. In your answer, you should:

- describe the main characteristics of the profile of your selected soil
- discuss how the factors identified above, except human activity, can influence these characteristics
- describe how human activity can alter soil characteristics

Total: 25 marks

■ ■ ■

Candidate's answer to Question 5

Below is an annotated diagram that shows the characteristics of a podzol.

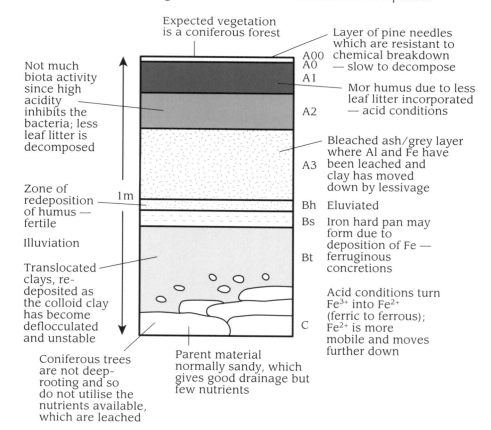

Expected vegetation is a coniferous forest

Not much biota activity since high acidity inhibits the bacteria; less leaf litter is decomposed

Zone of redeposition of humus — fertile

Illuviation

Translocated clays, re-deposited as the colloid clay has become deflocculated and unstable

Coniferous trees are not deep-rooting and so do not utilise the nutrients available, which are leached

Parent material normally sandy, which gives good drainage but few nutrients

A00
A0
A1 — Layer of pine needles which are resistant to chemical breakdown — slow to decompose

Mor humus due to less leaf litter incorporated — acid conditions

A2

A3 — Bleached ash/grey layer where Al and Fe have been leached and clay has moved down by lessivage

Bh Eluviated

Bs Iron hard pan may form due to deposition of Fe — ferruginous concretions

Bt

Acid conditions turn Fe^{3+} into Fe^{2+} (ferric to ferrous); Fe^{2+} is more mobile and moves further down

C

1 m

𝒆 The candidate has decided to describe the characteristics, for the first bullet point, using a diagram of a podzol profile. Although this is an 'essay' type question, there is no reason why, on physical topics such as this, candidates cannot present their information in this form (this would also be true for questions on plate tectonics, vulcanicity, earthquakes, vegetation successions etc.). In this case, we see an excellent example of how to describe a soil profile. There is plenty of information here, as the candidate clearly recognises the differences between, and details of, the various horizons. This part of the answer can therefore be credited at Level III. The diagram also contains material concerning the factors that influence these characteristics (second bullet point). Once the text has been read, the examiner can return to the diagram to see if it adds anything to what has been written. If so, more credit can be awarded.

The parent material, as I found when I carried out coursework on soils in Dean Clough Reservoir in Lancashire, is usually sandy. It has large particles of sand, which fit loosely and thus give large and many pore spaces, allowing good drainage. The drainage affects the pH of the soil, because it encourages leaching of metal cations in podzols, i.e. Al^{3+}, Fe^{2+}. The concentration of metal cations decreases, therefore increasing the concentration of hydrogen ions, and so making the soil more acidic. This removal of nutrients also affects the fertility and organic content of the soil as the drainage encourages lessivage; so clay becomes redeposited, or even lost to the parent material. If there are fewer clay–humus complexes available because they have been moved down through lessivage, there is less space on the micelle for water to adhere. This affects the moisture content of the soil and thus prevents it becoming water-logged and forming a gley.

The climate is normally cold and humid and one where precipitation is greater than evaporation. These cold conditions inhibit the soil biota as they prefer warmer conditions; therefore, less leaf litter is incorporated into the soil. This gives rise to humus of a mor type, allowing fewer clay–humus complexes and metal cations; thus, pH is reduced to an acid. All this precipitation helps to increase leaching of metal cations by water percolating through the soil and exchanging its hydrogen ions for metal cations. The metal cations are thus lost, but hydrogen ions are gained, leading to the increased acidity.

The coniferous woodland has pine trees that are not deep-rooted and so do not utilise the nutrients. Unused nutrients are easily leached by percolating water. The pine needles are waxy in coating and so do not break down easily. A build-up of dropped needles thus occurs and less organic matter is contributed, giving a lower organic content figure for the soil. This also gives rise to a low pH, since the less organic matter there is, the fewer clay–humus complexes there are, so there is less space for nutrients to adhere to and they are lost through leaching. This high acidity causes the colloidal clay to become unstable; it becomes deflocculated (it breaks up) and is easily moved down by lessivage as it becomes more mobile.

Time is needed to establish horizons in the soil and for vegetation to have an effect on its formation.

@ This response to the second bullet point is very good. The candidate examines the factors one by one and shows clearly how each one influences the podzol soil profile. There is a slight element of repetition in some of the material, particularly in reference to soil pH, but there is a definite attempt to show how much each factor contributes to the acidity of the soil. A great deal of detail is given regarding the effect of the processes and certainly, as far as it is possible with a question on soil characteristics, there seems to be some element of discussion in the way in which the material is presented. There is nothing on topography, but in the overall context of what is put forward this does not seem to detract from the quality of the answer. This material certainly qualifies to be assessed at Level III, where the criteria would be 'wide variety of factors identified with well-developed links and clear explanations'. The criteria for Level IV would be 'linkage of soil-forming factors together (for example climate to vegetation to organic content) and then to soil character'. Some of the material put forward could be considered to fulfil Level IV criteria, so this answer should be considered at least at the very top of Level III.

Irrigation can cause salinisation of the soil by adding saline nutrients. This increases pH (the soil becomes alkaline) and, eventually, unable to grow anything. This happened in El Sayeha near Ismalia in Egypt. Irrigation can also improve the water content of the soil, so it can provide more moisture for the vegetation.

Burning, as in burning of heather moorland for grouse farming in the Trough of Bowland in the Ribble Valley, causes nutrients to be released from the vegetation and they go back to the soil. However, after a long period of time, burning can remove all nutrients. You could also burn the soil, if you are not careful, by combusting the organic matter; this would result in a low pH and an infertile soil.

Liming (marling) or adding fertiliser can improve the soil's nutrient content, as can grazing, because animals contribute droppings (or manure). Extra nutrients are thus added to increase the pH.

@ After the quality shown in the material relating to the first two bullet points, this is a disappointing response. Considering the number of ways in which human activity can enhance or degrade soils by changing the soil characteristics, to give only three ideas, and very sketchily at that, certainly falls well short of the standard seen previously. The candidate was asked to discuss the statement with reference to either podzols or brown earths, but there is absolutely no reference to the chosen soil here. Podzols and irrigation is difficult to imagine, but even allowing for this, the material on irrigation is poor in that the process is seen as one that 'adds saline nutrients'. At this level, some explanation of how those nutrients are added is required, i.e. some reference to salts being drawn up the soil with the excess evaporated water. Indicating that adding water enables the soil to provide more to the vegetation seems to be scratching around for something to write! As there is no reference at all to podzols in this part of the answer, it is difficult for the examiner to see how to credit this material. However, there is some detail in the general material on offer and it is delivered with examples, so it is possible to credit this at the low end of Level II.

e Overall, there is much to credit in this answer, even allowing for the final part. This essay is certainly worth credit at Level III and towards the top end. The answer as a whole is well presented and organised in a clear and logical manner, with accurate use of English and geographical terminology. A number of examples are given, but not always in great detail. In terms of the quality of the material and the way in which the answer is put together, such an answer is worth 20 or 21 marks of the maximum 25.

Impact of climatic change and human activity on the vegetation of the British Isles

'Human activity has had a much greater impact on the climax vegetation of the British Isles than all the climate changes since the end of the last ice age.'

Discuss the extent to which you agree with this statement. In your answer, you should refer to examples and:
- describe the climate variations that have taken place since the retreat of the ice sheets and the resulting changes in vegetation
- discuss how human activity has altered climax vegetation
- assess the relative importance of climate change and human activity on the climax vegetation of the British Isles

Total: 25 marks

■ ■ ■

Candidate's answer to Question 6

Several climate variations have taken place since the retreat of the ice sheets. The last ice age ended around 13 000 years before present (BP) and coincided with the last major glaciation to affect the British Isles. As a result of the retreat, the associated vegetation developed into a tundra-type landscape, similar to that seen in northern Canada today. This was a sub-Arctic climate in which a tundra vegetation developed, including dwarf trees such as willow, as the climate warmed. Around 10 000 years BP, this developed into a boreal climate zone, with associated forests. This would have included hazel trees and the development of birch as the climate became warmer, drier and distinctly more continental. This period was cut short by the Loch Lomond readvance of the ice sheets around 7000 years BP, which meant that there was a return to glacial times and a tundra landscape. The Loch Lomond readvance was relatively short-lived and another warming in climate followed. This warmer and drier period saw the reintroduction of birch trees and associated vegetation. After this came the Atlantic period, around 4000 years BP, characterised by wetter conditions. With this came deciduous woodland, which we now consider to be our climatic climax vegetation.

After the Atlantic period, there was a gradual drying of the climate. This has generally continued to the present day, although there have been a few minor variations over the past 2000 years. At the time of William the Conqueror, the Domesday Book reported the presence of lime trees and even vineyards in England, with some of them stretching far north. There have also been occasions when the climate has been colder for short periods, such as in the eighteenth and nineteenth centuries when there were frost fairs on the River Thames. Recently, however, there has been a general global warming, which is thought to be due to emissions of greenhouse gases.

e The candidate shows some knowledge of the climatic changes that have occurred since the last ice age, although some of the chronology is not accurate enough for an answer at this level. The generally accepted sequence is: periglacial; warming into the allerod period (12°C in summer); pre-boreal (glacial advance) and boreal; Atlantic period with warm summers and mild winters, and wet; sub-boreal (warmer and drier); sub-Atlantic maritime. Then, from 2000 BP to the present day, there was a general gradual improvement, although colder and wetter following 1000 BP, until 450 BP, when there was a 'mini ice age' (AD 1540–1700). There are several inaccuracies in the candidate's account, particularly in reference to the timing of the 'mini ice ages'. There is not enough detail about the vegetation that developed under certain climatic conditions. The boreal, for example, had more than birch trees, and the candidate should have given more information on the Atlantic vegetation than simply deciduous forests. The Level II descriptor in the mark scheme for the first bullet point is 'some detailed variations in climate recognised, with the resulting changes in vegetation'. The descriptor for Level III is 'depth and accuracy in linking a range of climate changes to associated vegetation changes'. It is therefore clear that this material should be considered at least at Level II, and at the top end, but it is arguable whether the candidate shows the quality to reach Level III. Some of the statements regarding the change from the boreal into the Atlantic are good, but most examiners would prefer to see a little more detail before raising this answer into Level III.

When humans started to live in the British Isles, they were hunter/gatherers and so their action did not affect the deciduous woodland climax vegetation. There was some deforestation for firewood, but the fires that were started did not represent any hazard to the woodland. As the population grew, there was a change from the hunter/gatherer way of life to grazing and to arable farming. Large areas of woodland were cut down so that crops, particularly cereals, could be planted. This began to happen around 5000 BP in the Neolithic period. The last 2000 years have seen the growth of urban areas, particularly during the nineteenth and twentieth centuries. Urban building has meant that many areas have vanished under concrete and tarmac and have been unable to return to any form of vegetation.

In some upland areas, forests were removed and replaced eventually by heather moorland. This is often managed as a home for grouse, which are exploited by the shooting industry. An example of such an area is Otley Chase in West Yorkshire. Other areas were covered in wetlands and fens. The Norfolk Broads, for example, are maintained to stop the natural process of succession leading to the climatic climax community. Some deciduous forests have been removed and replaced by conifers for commercial exploitation, such as in the Lake District.

e There is an attempt to give some chronology here, in showing how humans have been responsible for the removal of the climax vegetation. This is better than simply giving a list of the purposes for which the vegetation has been removed, and satisfies the Level III descriptor which is 'breadth of human activities and their impact well described and put within a time scale'. Although vegetation types other than forest are mentioned, it is not clear that the candidate understands that there can be more than one climax vegetation, and that not all of the British Isles would be covered in deciduous forests if humans had not intervened.

Climate change has had an immense effect over a long period of time in changing the dominant vegetation of the British Isles, as conditions have become warmer or colder and drier or wetter. However, since about 6000 BP, humans have had a major impact on the vegetation as population numbers have increased. This human activity has given rise to the widespread changes in vegetation discussed above, leading to a plagioclimax in many areas of the British Isles, as opposed to the climatic climax community which might have occurred if developments had been entirely natural. It is certainly true to say that over the last 5000 years of the history of the British Isles, humans have had a far greater impact on the vegetation than has climate, which was the dominant factor in change before this period.

e There is an attempt here to assess the relative importance of climate and human intervention in changing the vegetation of the British Isles. The Level III descriptor for the last bullet point reads 'both sides are considered and a reasoned conclusion is reached'. This part of the answer is at the bottom end of this Level, since it only just satisfies these criteria.

e **Overall, this is a reasonable answer which, in places, shows that the candidate does have some understanding of the relative roles of climate and humans on the vegetation of the British Isles. Some of the material is good, but there is just not enough of it to take it above the lower end of Level III. The answer is well organised and presented (even allowing for the bullet points within the question), and the use of English is accurate. There are examples, but they are limited in number, range and details. This information, together with the quality of the geographical material, is enough for 17 or 18 marks out of 25.**

Physical hazards

'Geological activity is responsible for hazards which produce some extreme impacts in terms of loss of life and damage to property. If the consequences of such hazards are to be reduced, then appropriate management is necessary.'

Discuss the above statement with reference to either earthquakes or volcanoes. In your answer, you should refer to examples and:

- describe briefly how geological activity produces such extreme impacts
- show how the impact of earthquakes or volcanoes varies with the scale of the hazard and other factors
- discuss the management strategies used to reduce the impact of earthquakes or volcanoes
- assess the success of such management strategies

Total: 25 marks

■ ■ ■

Candidate's answer to Question 7

The Mexico City earthquake of 1985 was the result of geological activity. The remainder of the Cocos plate is still being forced under the North American plate by sea-floor spreading in the Pacific. The presence of a seismic gap, known as the Michacaon, meant that the area was free of small earthquakes and so pressure had been building up due to the lack of ability to release it. The resultant release of tension deep in the Benioff zone created massive shock waves which radiated to the surface. Although the epicentre was 2 km off the Mexican coast, the depth of the focus and the power generated by the movement meant that shockwaves were able to travel inland to Mexico City.

> ℯ This response to the first bullet point is of Level II standard. The candidate has written very specifically about one particular earthquake and has given exact details as to why the event took place. The plates involved, the direction in which one is moving, the evidence of the seismic gap and the location of the epicentre are all stated, which places it high in Level II. To reach Level III, it would be necessary to include more details of the relationship between the epicentre and Mexico City, and perhaps also explain the significance of the presence of a seismic gap.

The impact of an earthquake varies according to its force, which is measured on the Richter scale. Areas that are not in a seismic gap, such as parts of California, will have more frequent, but weaker, earthquakes. Earthquakes at the leading edges of plates will be more powerful than those at constructive margins, as more pressure is built up. Smaller earthquakes do little other than cause a slight tremor and some shaking of furniture. The Mexico City earthquake, however, was at a leading edge and in a seismic gap, so destruction was great.

A number of factors affect the damage that the earthquake brings about. The main problem for Mexico City was that it was built on a former lake bed, so the silt and peat allowed water particles to move between them as they were 'excited' by the low frequencies of the shock waves. This resulted in the ground behaving like a liquid (liquefaction). When this happens, the ground is unable to hold the weight of the buildings and so they sink into the ground. The shockwaves and liquefaction were allowed to cause further damage because of the natural frequency of the peat and silt that the city was built upon; this resulted in prolonged shaking, causing major damage. The intervals of pressure release that are characteristic of a seismic gap also prolonged the shaking, which led to further damage.

On the human side, there was a lack of money and corruption within the city government, which meant that building regulations were often ignored. Foundations of buildings had often not gone deep enough to reach a more solid base and so many buildings collapsed easily during the earthquake.

In large urban areas such as Mexico City, secondary factors are made worse. The rupturing of electricity cables and gas mains causes fires which burn down many buildings. Water supplies are disrupted, meaning that fire crews are unable to fight the fires that have been generated. Disease can also occur as the water supply becomes contaminated; this is coupled with the inability of medical services to cope with the first phase of the earthquake as it is likely that many medical facilities have been destroyed. In Mexico City, the many shanty towns built on steep slopes collapsed, as a result of a combination of shaking and landslides. As these areas were densely populated, there was a huge loss of life.

> ✐ This is excellent material in response to the second bullet point. The candidate has introduced the idea of secondary impacts and has tried to show how both the physical force of the earthquake and human factors are responsible for determining the extent of the impact. All of this has been put into the context of the Mexico City earthquake. Identifying primary and secondary factors puts such material within Level II of the mark scheme as the candidate has introduced some idea of classification (along with identifying human and physical factors), and the detail with which this has been presented would certainly qualify for Level III. Points are also linked in a way that shows the candidate has a very clear idea of what determines the impact of an earthquake, while the answer looks closely at scale and other factors. All of this reveals a clear understanding on the part of the candidate, placing this part of the answer at Level IV.

The management strategies in Mexico City were poor. In California, however, risk assessment has reduced serious damage. For example, builders are required by law to reinforce structures with steel, and estate agencies must inform buyers if a property lies on a fault line. The idea of using strong, flexible steel means that the building can sway with the earthquake. It can also be insisted upon that foundations are located within bedrock, so reducing the risk of buildings collapsing. A new idea, seen in a different context at the Bridgewater Hall in Manchester, is to mount buildings on springs and shock-absorbers to reduce shaking.

Prevention cannot be complete, so early warning strategies have been attempted. Palaeoseismology investigates ancient earthquakes by analysing the surface profile and trying to guess when the next earthquake will strike. This may enable scientists to give a general warning, but it is impossible to predict accurately the occurrence of an earthquake event. Remote-sensing can be used to investigate bulges in the ground which might suggest seismic activity. Even research into animal reactions has been carried out in China, in an attempt to establish some form of prediction. The levels of gases (e.g. radon) emitted before events have been researched, as have the levels of water in wells. Such short-term predictions have had limited success. Even if they were successful, there is no way that large-scale evacuation could be contemplated, particularly where large squatter settlements are involved.

Many governments in earthquake-prone areas have been looking at ways to prepare the people for hazard events. People need to be told what to do and where to go in an emergency. They need to be advised as to what to stock, in order to be ready. This would cover such things as first-aid kits, food, water purification tablets and torches. Education is important — earthquake drills are taught regularly in schools in areas such as Japan and California.

As can be seen, it is extremely difficult to predict this hazard, both in terms of time and magnitude. Therefore, evacuation, probably the safest option, is impossible at the present time. Scientists, though, are continually developing more accurate and effective methods, so, hopefully, the impact of earthquakes can be considerably reduced.

🄴 This is another excellent section. The candidate covers a number of strategies and is prepared to discuss their implementation by trying to put them into the contexts of before and after the event. The success of the strategies is assessed, thus dealing with the third and fourth bullet points together. The candidate has got it right here. This gives a much more fluid text and avoids certain areas of repetition that would have occurred had the strategies been separated from an assessment of how successful they had been. There is also good use of examples which, although not in any great depth, do complement the general points that have been made. Again, this should be credited at the very highest point of Level III. Indeed, the strategies are so well linked to an assessment of success that a mark within Level IV could be considered.

🄴 Overall, this is an excellent answer. It is well presented and organised in a logical manner (even allowing for the bullet points given in the question), and with accurate use of English. There is good use of exemplar material, particularly that on Mexico City, but the candidate also widens the range by making reference to other areas that are prone to the earthquake hazard. This deserves at least 23 marks out of 25.

The tropical regions of Africa with wet and dry seasons

'There has been debate over the origin of the vegetation of the tropical regions of Africa with wet and dry seasons. For some it is viewed as a natural response to the seasonal changes that take place in the climate of this area, whereas for others it is regarded as a product of human interference over the last 2000 years.'

Discuss this statement. In your answer you should:
- identify the main features of the natural vegetation and the climate of this area
- describe the ways in which the vegetation is adapted to the seasonal climate of this area
- discuss the importance of human activity on the vegetation of this area

Total: 25 marks

■ ■ ■

Candidate's answer to Question 8

The vegetation of the savanna grasslands is linked closely to the climate of that area. It is an area with alternate wet and dry seasons. For some of the year, there are heavy rains caused by the migration of the ITCZ, following the overhead sun. This usually takes place in June in the northern hemisphere and December in the southern hemisphere. From now on I will refer all of my answer to the northern hemisphere and to the area around Kano in northern Nigeria. For the rest of the year, the weather is very dry; there is no or little rain. This is caused by the movement away of the overhead sun and the ITCZ and the movement over Kano of the subtropical high-pressure area. The air in this is subsiding, causing little rain to be produced as clouds are rare. The weather is hot all year round, but especially so just before the onset of the rainy season. In the dry season, because clouds are rare, the temperature can drop to near freezing at night.

In the more equatorial areas, the savanna vegetation consists of very tall grasses — up to 2 metres in height. Within this grassland, there are many trees dotted about, producing a parkland-like environment. In the drier areas, nearer to the desert margins, shorter grasses appear, with bare soil in between. This is often where drought-resistant trees are found, like the acacia and the boabab tree (which stores water in its trunk).

The vegetation is adapted to the climate seasons in a number of ways. Firstly, the trees are deciduous, losing their leaves in the dry season, although some evergreens are also found. They have hard, leathery leaves to reduce water losses through transpiration. Many of the trees and bushes have very small leaves to reduce transpiration. Indeed, there are thorny bushes, which act as small-leaved plants; thus reducing water loss.

The acacia is well adapted to the dry environment. It has an umbrella shape to its upper branches which shades the root areas, thus reducing evaporation from the ground. The roots then extend widely to collect as much water as possible; the tree also has a deep tap root which can reach groundwater supplies. The boabab tree is also well adapted to the environment. It is known as the 'upside-down tree' because it has a very thick trunk and only a small collection of upper branches. It, too, has a huge set of roots underground. The trunk of the tree is able to store water in its fleshy interior during times of drought, and the thick bark reduces water loss, as well as being fire-resistant.

There are other ways in which the vegetation is adapted to the climate. Much of the grass dies back during the dry season to regrow quickly when the summer rains come. Many of these grasses grow in tussocks to withstand the strong, desiccating (drying) winds blowing across the wide open plains. Cacti can be found in the desert areas; they also store water in their fleshy interiors.

So, there are many ways in which the vegetation is adapted to the seasonal climate of the area. However, some people believe that the main reason for the vegetation structure in such areas is the action of humans, in particular grazing and burning. Such people argue that the boabab and acacia trees are the dominant trees in the region because they are pyrophytic — they do not burn, due to their fire-resistant barks. Also, grazing animals eat the grasses, causing them to regrow, and stop other trees from growing by eating the young shoots. The acacia and the boabab trees have survived because they have thorns and needles, which animals will not eat.

I believe that the reason for the nature of the vegetation in this area is more likely to be related to the climate, with the impact of human beings reinforcing the situation created by nature. The vegetation has clear links to the climate, and clear adaptations, just as the vegetation of the rainforests is adapted to the climate of those areas. I think it is unlikely that the actions of humans alone could create the sort of landscape that is widespread around the Nigerian city of Kano — the tropical savanna grasslands.

@ The candidate has, on the whole, followed the structure provided by the bullet points, providing good detail for some sections, but not for others. In the first paragraph of the answer, additional material is provided that is not required. The first bullet point asks for a basic description of the vegetation and climate. As is often the case, the candidate attempts to provide reasons for the climate, with references to the ITCZ and high-pressure areas, but no precise detail is offered concerning the climate; all we are given are vague words such as 'hot', 'wet' and 'dry'. More detail of temperatures, rainfall amounts and latitudinal or seasonal variations are required to access the higher marking levels. Reference to the soil moisture budget would also have been relevant. The following paragraphs are better. Detail is offered of heights of plants, names of species (the mis-spelling of baobab is remarkably common), and good accounts of plant adaptations are given. The approach of referring to specific adaptations by specific plants is a good one to adopt. Other adaptations could have been offered, but this answer clearly enters Level III at this stage. Further detail could also have been given about local variations, for example the differences between those areas alongside temporary river courses and those well away from such areas. The paragraph concerning the impact of human activities is brief, but the general ideas are correct. Detail on the probable causes of fires (human or natural) could have been offered, with more detail of how the fire resistance, or fire tolerance, of both trees and grasses actually operates. The final paragraph is a weak evaluative summative comment which consists of personal opinion rather than geographical evidence.

Mark scheme

G	Level I, 0–6	Level II, 7–12	Level III, 13–17	Level IV, 18–20
	Simple statements of vegetation and climate characteristics	More detailed material on characteristics, e.g. names of species, accurate figures of climate	Well developed detail, e.g. latitudinal variations or other local variations	
	Limited account of adaptations — simple statements of facts, e.g. long roots, thick barks	More detailed analysis of adaptations, often linked to individual species and to specific aspects of the climate	Well developed detail of adaptations; analysis of the variety of ways in which certain species adapt to drought and heat, and how these vary locally	
		Analysis of the ways in which one human activity has influenced the vegetation	Development of effects of human activity (has it worked with the climate or against it?) with the possible analysis of more than one activity	Good evaluative comments on opening statement given in question, i.e. climate versus human activity
S	Level I, 0–1	Level II, 2–3	Level III, 4–5	
	Information is adequately organised and presented with reasonably accurate use of English	Well organised and presented with accurate use of English; limited examples	Well organised and presented in a clear and logical manner, with very accurate use of English; range of examples	

Overall, this answer is awarded 15 marks (Level III) for the geography (G) and 3 marks for skills (S); a total of 18 marks.

Conflict over the use of resources

On a clear summer's day, it is hard to imagine a more idyllic place than Lingarabay on the island of Harris in the Western Isles of Scotland. Meadows of ferns and lilies run down to the edge of a cove etched into the rocky shoreline. Buzzards and herons fly overhead. Rising above is the mass of Roineabhal mountain, covered in heather.

But, if an English quarry company has its way, Lingarabay will not remain a beautiful place for much longer. It wants to develop a superquarry to excavate the massive reserves of hard rock which make up the mountain, in order to meet the demands of road builders and cement makers throughout the British Isles and Europe.

Population of Harris

Year	Population
1931	4500
1951	3990
1971	2880
1991	2140

Likely economic impact of the superquarry

Years from start of scheme	Number of persons employed	Annual cash injection into local economy
0–5	210	£1.3 million
6–10	245	£2.2 million
11+	230	£3.5 million

Some socioeconomic aspects, 1991

	Harris	Scotland
Proportion of second holiday homes (%)	13	2
Decline in school rolls 1981–91 (%)	27	4
People competing for each job vacancy	28	11
Average per capita income (£)	3250	5000

Write an account of the conflict on the island of Harris, Scotland, as detailed above. In your answer, you should:
- identify both the proposal that led to the conflict and the main participants in it
- discuss the attitudes of the participants to the issues that have arisen in the conflict over the use of the resource
- describe and explain the processes that may operate to resolve the conflict

Total: 25 marks

■ ■ ■

Candidate's answer to Question 9

The conflict on this beautiful Scottish island is being caused by the proposed development by an English quarry company to excavate massive reserves of hard rock for road-building purposes and cement-making. Clearly, the company is in favour of the proposal as it will seek to maximise the profit that it can make from digging out the rock, but other people, such as environmentalists and locals, will be against it.

There will be others who have a view on the proposal, including the unemployed on the island (particularly school leavers). Shopkeepers and pub landlords, people who have moved to the island and bought second homes there, and no doubt governments, both local and national, will have an opinion on the issue. These people are known as participants in the conflict and each will have a standpoint.

As I said earlier, the English quarry company will be in favour of the development. Roads are being built all the time in the UK, including Scotland, and the materials for such construction have to be found somewhere. The company probably feels that here is a ready-made supply of huge quantities that they can excavate and ship out without disturbing large numbers of people. A port could be built to accommodate ships to move the rock to other parts of Britain; a road link is more unlikely, as the island of Harris is in a remote part of the UK. The company has done some preliminary research and found out that jobs will be created — over 200 for at least the next 11 years, which on a small island of just over 2000 people is a huge number of newly created jobs. Not only that, the company says that the economic impact of the superquarry will be substantial, rising to over £3 million a year after 11 years from the start of the scheme. The company will obviously think that no-one in the local area will be against the scheme.

The local council of the island will be in favour. They will value the number of jobs created, especially in an area where the population has more than halved since 1930. They will also welcome the input of new wealth into the area — the cash injection will go into new roads, other social facilities such as leisure centres, and even into sponsorship of schools. The multiplier effect will come into play — investment brings further investment, and the whole will become better off as a result.

The Scottish Parliament should also be in favour. Lingarabay on Harris is a very remote and backward area (as shown by the low incomes — 65% of the Scottish average), and the investment by the English company will be good for the area. However, there will be some members of the Scottish Parliament, especially Scottish Nationalists, who will see that the company is English, and will object to the English taking away Scottish resources; they may well be against the proposal for political reasons.

The local people on the island will have mixed views. The older generation will probably be against the development as they will see great changes in the area caused by heavy lorries, noise pollution, dust and dirt. However, there is a greater number of people competing for jobs in this area, and many of these will be school leavers, even though the number on school rolls is declining. Unemployed people will be in favour of the quarry, as jobs will be created.

The people who will be against the scheme will include environmentalists. These people challenge any new development in a scenic area such as this. They will not want pollution of any sort — visual, air or water. Conservationists have a similar view, and will not want to see large meadows of ferns and lilies destroyed. They will also want to preserve the habitats of the buzzards and herons.

A relatively large number of people own a second home in the area. They will have retired to the area, wanting to escape the hustle and bustle of the city. Some may also have homes in Glasgow and Edinburgh, and have bought a second home to have holidays in. These people will not want to have invested money in property that will lose value when quarry excavation starts.

So, how will this conflict be resolved? There are two ways: market processes and planning processes. In market processes, the highest bidder wins. In this case, it is likely that the English company will offer incentives to the locals and the local council, and even the Scottish Parliament, to allow it to excavate the rock. Any involvement of financial sweeteners by industry is a form of market process. It is more likely, though, that in this case planning procedures will have to be implemented. As there will be people for and against, an enquiry will be set up by the local council. People will be encouraged to put forward their arguments for and against, and the council will make a decision. After this, people can ask for an appeal to a High Court, or something similar, where lawyers put forward the same type of arguments, and once again the judge will make a decision. Each of these takes time, but at least the system is democratic. I have already said that the members of the Scottish Parliament are likely to have a view on such a massive scheme, so it is likely that the development will be discussed there, bringing in wider political opinions such as the Scots versus the English. But at the end of all of these processes, a final decision will be made, perhaps by the Prime Minister of Scotland.

🖉 The candidate has more or less followed the structure provided by the bullet points. However, the answer starts in a very generalised manner. The first paragraph is very simple in its ideas and structure, and does not extend beyond Level I. A common failing in such questions is to identify participants in a very generalised way. Answers need to be far more specific, such as bird-watchers instead of environmentalists, and shopkeepers instead of locals. Once the participants have been identified clearly, it becomes easier to attribute attitudes. The candidate does therefore attain Level II in the second paragraph for a more detailed identification of some of the participants in the conflict. The third paragraph, concerning the quarry company, is much better. Here, the attitudes of the company are discussed well, with good use being made of the data. Level III is reached. The following paragraphs, concerning the local council and the Scottish Parliament, are also well argued, each reaching Level III. The next paragraph, regarding local people, is less effective, with a return to simplistic arguments. The following paragraph examines a more specific group which is against the proposal — conservationists. However, the discussion of attitudes is not strong enough for Level III. More depth concerning the damaging of habitats is required — as it stands, the answer has simply been lifted from the data. The penultimate paragraph, concerning second home-owners, is better, and achieves Level III. The final paragraph consists of a good summary of planning procedures, with a fleeting comment regarding market processes. Some of the detail may be incorrect (it is the *First Minister* of Scotland, not the Prime Minister), but the general comments concerning public enquiries, appeals and further appeals to higher bodies are reasonably correct in this context. Once again, the answer reaches Level III.

Mark scheme

G	Level I, 0–6	Level II, 7–12	Level III, 13–17	Level IV, 18–20
	Simple statements of the causes of the conflict, with generalised naming of participants	More detailed statements on the causes of the conflict, clearly linked to a named area studied; participants are clearly identified	Thorough account of the causes of the conflict, with background material being provided on the area and/or participants	
		Brief statements of attitudes both for and against the issues; statements tend to be very generalised	Attitudes clearly attributed to identified participants in the conflict; some recognition of variation in the basis of attitudes within groups which may lose or benefit from the conflict	Recognition of variation in attitudes over time and/or according to the outcome of the conflict
	Simple outline of the processes and procedures which operate to resolve the conflict	Detailed description of the processes operating to resolve the conflict	Analysis of the various processes that may operate to resolve the conflict; some statement of success	
S	Level I, 0–1	Level II, 2–3	Level III, 4–5	
	Information is adequately organised and presented, with reasonably accurate use of English	Well organised and presented, with accurate use of English; limited examples	Well organised and presented in a clear and logical manner, with very accurate use of English; range of examples	

ℓ Overall, the answer reaches the upper limit of Level III for the geography (G) — 17 marks — and scores 4 marks for the skills (S); a total of 21 marks.

AS Geography
UNIT 1

AQA

Specification B

Module 1: The Dynamics of Change

David Redfern & Malcolm Skinner

Philip Allan Updates
Market Place
Deddington
Oxfordshire
OX15 0SE

Tel: 01869 338652
Fax: 01869 337590
e-mail: sales@philipallan.co.uk
www.philipallan.co.uk

ISBN 0 86003 457 7

This Guide has been written specifically to support students preparing for the
AQA Specification B AS Geography Unit 1 examination. The content has been
neither approved nor endorsed by AQA and remains the sole responsibility of
the authors.

Typeset by Magnet Harlequin, Oxford
Printed by Information Press, Eynsham, Oxford

Contents

Introduction

Content Guidance

Questions and Answers

Introduction

About this guide

Students of Advanced Subsidiary (AS) geography who are following the AQA Specification B all have to study **Module 1: The Dynamics of Change**, which forms the content of Unit 1. They will be seeking to understand:

- the key ideas of the content of the module;
- the nature of the assessment material by the consideration of sample structured questions;
- the requirements to answer successfully the above questions;
- how to perform well in examinations generally.

This guide provides opportunities to satisfy each of the above requirements.

This Introduction provides an explanation of some of the key command words used in examination papers, together with guidance on how to answer questions requiring extended prose. There is also advice concerning geographical skills, and learning and revision techniques.

The Content Guidance section summarises the essential information of Module 1. It is designed to make you aware of the material that has to be covered and learnt. In particular, the meaning of key terms is made clear.

The Question and Answer section provides sample questions and candidate responses at the C/D grade boundary and at the A/B grade boundary. Each answer is followed by a detailed examiner's response. It is suggested that you read through the relevant topic area in the Content Guidance section before attempting a question from the Question and Answer section, and only read the specimen answers after you have tackled the question yourself.

Examination skills

Command terms used in AS geography examinations

One of the major problems that you face in any examination is your difficulty in interpreting the demands of the questions asked of you. Thorough revision is essential, but you also require an awareness of what is expected from you in the examination itself. Too often candidates attempt to answer the question they think is there, or that they have been prepared for, rather than the one that is actually set. Answering an examination question is challenging enough, without the extra self-inflicted handicap of misreading the question.

Correct interpretation of the command words of a question is therefore very important. In an AS geography examination paper, a variety of command words are used. Certain command words demand more of the candidate than others: some require a simple task to be performed; others require greater intellectual thought and a longer response. The notes below offer advice on the main command words that are used.

(1) Identify... What...? Name... State... Give...

These words ask for brief answers to a simple task, such as:

- a landform may be identified from a photograph
- a value from a graph is required
- a named example of a feature is required

You are not advised to answer by using a single word. It is always better to write a short sentence incorporating the answer required.

(2) Define... Explain the meaning of... What is meant by...? Outline...

These words ask for a relatively short answer, usually two or three sentences, where the precise meaning of a term is required. The use of an example is often helpful. The size of the mark allocation will give an indication of the length of answer required.

(3) Describe...

This is one of the most widely used command words. A verbal picture of the distinctive features of the item to be described is required. The account should be factual, *without any attempt to explain*. Usually the examiner will give some clue as to what particular aspect of the description is required. Some examples are given below.

Describe the characteristics of...

For example, in the case of a landform the following sub-questions may be useful in writing the answer:

- what does it look like?
- what is it made of?
- how big is it?
- where is it in relation to other features?

Describe the changes in...

This command often relates to a graph, or a table. Good use of accurate adverbs is required here, using words such as rapidly, steeply, gently, slightly, greatly etc.

Describe the differences between...

Here *only* differences between two sets of data will be credited. It is better if these are presented in the form of a series of separate sentences, each identifying one difference. Writing a paragraph on one item, followed by a paragraph on another item, makes the examiner complete the task on your behalf.

Describe the relationship between...

Here *only* the links between two sets of data will be credited. It is important, therefore, that you establish the relationship clearly in verbal form, and that the link is explicitly stated. In most cases the relationship will be either a positive (direct) one or a negative (inverse) one.

Describe the distribution of...

This is usually used in conjunction with a map or set of maps. A description of the location of high concentrations of a variable is required, together with a similar description of those areas with a lower concentration. Better answers will also tend to identify anomalous areas or areas that go against an overall trend in the distributions, for example an area of high concentration in an area of predominantly low concentration.

(4) Compare...

You have to provide a point-by-point account of the similarities and differences between two sets of information or two areas. Two separate accounts do not comprise a comparison, and you will be penalised if you present two such accounts and expect the examiner to do the comparison on your behalf. A good technique would be to use comparative adjectives, for example larger than, smaller than, more steep than, less gentle than etc. Note that 'compare' refers to similarities *and* differences, whereas the command word 'contrast' just asks for differences.

(5) Explain... Suggest reasons for... How might...? Why...?

These commands ask for a statement as to why something occurs. The command word is testing your ability to know or understand why or how something happens. Such questions tend to carry a large number of marks, and you will be expected to write a relatively long piece of extended prose. It is important that you present a logical account which is both relevant and well organised.

(6) Using only an annotated diagram... With the aid of a diagram...

Here you *must* draw a diagram, and in the former case provide only a diagram. Annotations are labels that provide some additional description and/or explanation of the main features of the diagram. For example, in the case of a hydrograph (see p. 20) the identification of 'a rising limb' would constitute a label, whereas 'a steep rising limb caused by an impermeable ground surface' would form an annotation.

Developing extended prose-writing skills

Unit 1 contains some questions that will require lengthy written responses. These are not the essays that will be met at A2, but are called extended prose questions. They will form one of the most difficult aspects of the examination paper, but you must appreciate that this can be an opportunity for you to demonstrate how good you can be.

There is a set procedure for writing pieces of extended prose, which this section seeks to explain. First of all, you must have a plan of what you are going to write — in your head or on paper — before you start. All pieces of extended prose must have a beginning (introduction), a middle (argument) and an end (conclusion).

(1) The introduction
This must be there, but it does not have to be too long. It can be only one, or a few, sentences. It could provide a definition of terms given in the question, it could set the scene for the argument to follow or it could be a brief statement of an idea/concept/viewpoint that you are going to develop in the main body of your answer.

(2) The argument
This will form the main element of your answer and so will appear as a series of paragraphs. It is better if each paragraph develops one point only, but fully. Try to avoid paragraphs that list information without any depth or breadth to your answer. Also avoid answers where you put down all you know about a particular topic without any link to the actual question set. Make good use of examples — name real places (which could be local to you). Make them count by giving accurate detail which applies to the examples specifically, rather than to 'any town' or 'any place'.

(3) The conclusion
In an extended prose answer the conclusion should not be too long. Make sure it reiterates the main points stated in the introduction, but now supported by the evidence and facts given in the argument.

Should you produce plans of extended prose in the examination?
If you produce a plan at all, it must be brief, taking only 2–3 minutes to write, and it is suggested that this should be completed not on the examination paper itself but on a spare piece of paper. The plan must reflect the above formula — make sure you stick to it. Be logical, and only give an outline — retain the examples in your head, and include them at the most appropriate point in your answer.

Other aspects of writing extended prose
Always keep an eye on the time. Make sure you write clearly and concisely. Do not provide confused answers, or have endless sentences, or fail to use paragraphs. Above all, **read the question and answer the question**.

Geographical skills

Candidates for Unit 1 will be expected to have undertaken some investigative work, including fieldwork. This work must be based on a minimum of two hypotheses or research questions. Consequently there will be occasions when the following skills and practical techniques are assessed within the unit.

Identifying, collecting, selecting and using salient information

Sampling procedures.

Fieldwork, including the collection and use of primary sources:
- morphological maps, land-use maps, weather maps
- census returns
- observations
- questionnaires, interviews
- measurement of physical characteristics in a physical environment

The use of secondary sources:
- texts, published data
- OS and other maps at a variety of scales
- photographs
- information and communication technology, remotely sensed imagery and geographical information systems
- scanning, selection and abstraction

Organising, recording and presenting evidence

Graphs:
- histograms, line graphs (including those with logarithmic scales)
- pie graphs, bar graphs
- long- and cross-sections
- scatter diagrams (including trend lines), Lorenz curves and triangular graphs

Maps:
- isopleth maps
- choropleth maps
- sketch maps

Tables and written text.

Describing, analysing, evaluating and interpreting evidence

Map and photograph interpretation.

The application of descriptive statistical techniques:
- measures of central tendency (mean, mode and median)

Geographical relationships and changes in them:
- Spearman rank

The analysis of text:
- summary
- hypothesis formulation
- decision-making

The limitations of evidence and of conclusions drawn.

Techniques for learning and revision

The aim here is to suggest ways to revise material for Unit 1 and to provide ideas for increasing your ability to absorb, retain and recall factual information. They cannot all work for you, so choose only those techniques that seem to work best. Whichever techniques you choose, make sure you use them regularly.

Mind mapping

This is useful when trying to learn new information or when trying to pull together material from a range of different areas.

For an example of this technique, look at the mind map relating to river erosion below. Start off with the term 'river erosion' in the centre of a piece of paper and ring it. Then perform a personal brainstorm of the major forms of river erosion (abrasion, attrition etc.) and place these around the edge of the ring, like branches, as shown. Then, from each branch, add points which elaborate upon the initial term, with further subdivisions if necessary. This logical breaking down of the content helps you to assemble the main points that may influence the process of river erosion, and could assist in the writing of an examination answer on the topic.

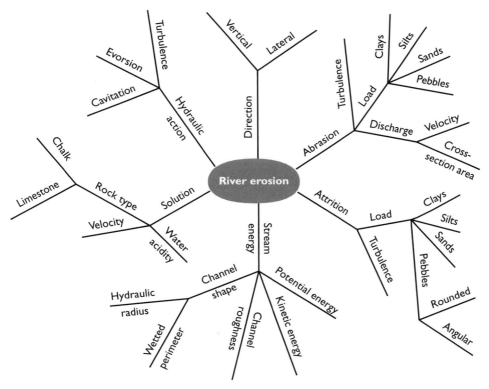

A mind map relating to river erosion

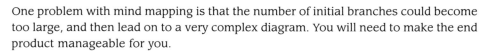
One problem with mind mapping is that the number of initial branches could become too large, and then lead on to a very complex diagram. You will need to make the end product manageable for you.

Each mind map is very personal to you, and should enable you to remember the key points in a topic and to concentrate on them more quickly.

Pictorial notes

Some people have the ability to remember facts according to where they are located on a page of notes — they can be said to have a 'photographic memory'. Others exhibit a variation of this by remembering colours, and what facts are contained within different coloured areas of their notes.

Another aspect of this form of revision is to convert written notes into a sketch or picture, and to use this as a revision tool. An example of this would be for you to draw a diagram of an anticyclone with subsiding air, and to add the characteristics of its weather (in either winter or summer — see p. 18) onto it. In this way you have a picture of its characteristics, together with descriptive annotations.

Fact cards

A more traditional way to learn material is the fact card approach. Here you buy a number of small cards from a stationery shop, and write your own summary of the key points of a particular topic onto the cards. One exercise that you could do is to transfer the contents of one A4 sheet of notes onto one card. The card(s) can then be carried round with you for reading during moments when you would otherwise be doing little, for example when travelling to school or sitting in a common room. Maintain your cards in a logical order using a treasury tag.

Mnemonics and acronyms

These are 'pegs' on which you can hang specific memories. You can use either letters or words to construct a mnemonic. One favourite helps you remember the rivers that drain into the River Ouse in Yorkshire: 'Sheffield United never won a cup did they?' — SUNWACDT. This translates to: Swale, Ure, Nidd, Wharfe, Aire, Calder, Don, Trent. Mnemonics where the initial letters make up a word are called acronyms. As with mind maps, the use of these can be, and possibly should be, personal to you.

Systems diagrams

The flow diagram of basin hydrology on p. 19 is an example of a systems diagram. This approach is probably very familiar to you. It records inputs and outputs, and shows movement by means of simple directional arrows.

Try to use this approach to summarise the impacts of demographic changes in urban areas within the UK. The inputs would be the specified changes over time, and the outputs would be their effects on the size, type and location of housing developments.

Skeleton lists

This is perhaps the most basic of ways to assemble ideas in a logical order before completing the task of writing an answer. Most topics in geography have a list of considerations that can be referred to when looking at factors affecting them.

For example, when considering the location of manufacturing industry (see p. 32), the following may apply:

Physical factors	Human factors
Raw materials	Labour
Power	Capital
Amount of land	Markets
Site of factory	Transport
	Government policies

These lists provide the skeleton around which a discussion of the location of any manufacturing industry could be constructed.

Content Guidance

This section provides an overview of the key terms and concepts covered in **Module 1: The Dynamics of Change**.

The content of Module 1 falls into three main areas.

(1) Physical geography: shorter term and local change
This involves the study of some aspects of British weather (depressions and anti-cyclones), and hydrological and geomorphological processes that operate within drainage basins in the British Isles.

(2) People and the environment: population and resources
This involves the study of environmental and social issues resulting from the imbalance between population and resources both in less economically developed countries (LEDCs) and in more economically developed countries (MEDCs). This leads on to a further analysis of specific issues associated with the use of energy resources in such countries.

(3) Human geography: changes in the UK in the last 30 years
This involves the study of changes in industry within the country, particularly those affecting manufacturing industry and services. Social and demographic changes within urban areas are also studied, with particular emphasis on geographical segregation based upon wealth, age and ethnicity.

Physical geography

Weather changes associated with the passage of a depression

	Cold front		Weather element	Warm front		
In the rear	*At passage*	*Ahead*		*In the rear*	*At passage*	*Ahead*
Continuous steady rise	Sudden rise	Steady or slight fall	**Pressure**	Steady or slight fall	Fall stops	Continuous fall
Veering to NW. Decreasing speed	Sudden veer, SW to W. Increase in speed, with squalls	SW, but increasing in speed	**Wind**	Steady SW. Constant	Sudden veer, S to SW	Slight backing ahead of front. Increase in speed
Little change	Significant drop	Slight fall, especially if raining	**Temperature**	Little change	Marked rise	Steady, little change
Variable in showers but usually low	Decreases sharply	Steady	**Humidity**	Little change	Rapid rise, often to near saturation	Gradual increase
Very good	Poor in rain, but quickly improves	Often poor	**Visibility**	Little change	Poor, often fog/mist	Good at first, but deteriorates rapidly
Shower clouds, clear skies and cumulus clouds	Heavy cumulonimbus	Low stratus and stratocumulus	**Clouds**	Overcast, stratus and stratocumulus	Low nimbostratus	Becoming increasingly overcast, cirrus to altostratus to nimbostratus
Bright intervals and scattered showers	Heavy rain, hail and thunderstorms	Light rain, drizzle	**Precipitation**	Light rain, drizzle	Rain stops or reverts to drizzle	Light rain, becoming more continuous and heavy

Key points

- A depression is an area of relatively low atmospheric pressure.
- It is represented on a weather map by a system of closed isobars with pressures decreasing towards the centre.
- Depressions usually move rapidly from west to east across the British Isles.

- Isobars are usually close together, producing a steep pressure gradient from the centre to the outer edges.
- Hence winds are often strong and generally flow inwards.
- In the British Isles the winds flow anticlockwise around the centre of the depression.
- Areas in the southern British Isles will often experience a change of wind direction from south to southwest to west to northwest — the wind is said to **veer**.
- Areas in the northern British Isles will often experience a change of wind direction from southeast to east to northeast to north — the wind is said to **back**.

Stage 1 A wave forms on polar front. Cloud and rain occur. Pressure falls.

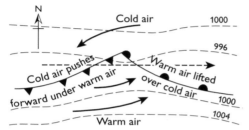

Key

— — — — —	Isobars (pressure in millibars)
——————→	Wind direction
▓▓▓▒▒░░¦¦¦¦	Main cloud and rain areas
------→	Movement of depression
▼——▼——	Cold front
●——●——	Warm front
●▼●▼●▼	Occluded front (cold catches up warm)

Stage 2 Winds blow round depression. Pressure falls. Cold front moves faster than warm front.

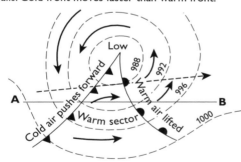

Stage 3 Cold front catches up warm front. Pressure rises. Depression starts to die as no warm air to lift near centre of low.

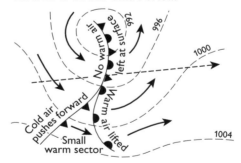

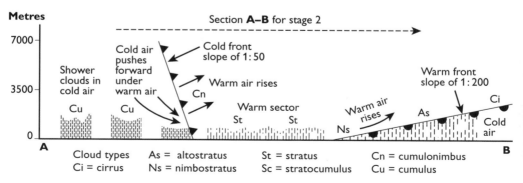

Section **A–B** for stage 2

Cloud types	As = altostratus	St = stratus	Cn = cumulonimbus
Ci = cirrus	Ns = nimbostratus	Sc = stratocumulus	Cu = cumulus

The stages of a depression

Formation

A depression affecting the British Isles originates in the north Atlantic where two different air masses meet along the Polar Front. An **air mass** is a large body of air in which there is only a gradual horizontal change in temperature and humidity. The two air masses involved are:

- polar maritime air — air from the northwest Atlantic, which is cold, dense and moist;
- tropical maritime air — air from the southwest, which is warmer, less dense and also moist.

These two bodies of air move towards each other, with the warmer, less dense air from the south rising above the colder, more dense air from the north. The rising air is removed by strong upper atmosphere winds (known as a jet stream), but as it rises it twists as its movement is affected by the earth's rotational spin. This twisting vortex causes a wave to be produced in the Polar Front at ground level, which increases in size to become a depression.

Two separate parts of the original front have now developed:

- the **warm front** — at the leading edge of the depression, where warmer, less dense air rises over the colder air ahead;
- the **cold front** — at the rear of the depression, where colder, more dense air pushes against the warmer air ahead of it.

In between these two fronts lies the **warm sector** — an area of warm and moist air. As the depression moves eastwards, the cold front gradually overtakes the warm front to form an **occlusion** in which the warmer air is lifted off the ground.

Anticyclonic weather conditions in winter and summer

Key points

- An anticyclone is an area of relatively high atmospheric pressure.
- It is represented on a weather map by a system of closed isobars with pressures increasing towards the centre.
- Anticyclones move slowly and may remain stationary over an area for several days and weeks.
- The air in an anticyclone subsides, that is, it falls from above. This therefore warms as it falls, producing a decrease in the relative humidity of the air. This in turn leads to a lack of cloud development, and dry conditions.
- Isobars are usually far apart, and therefore there is little pressure difference between the centre and edges of the anticyclone.
- Hence winds are weak and flow gently outwards.
- In the British Isles the winds flow clockwise around the centre of the anti-cyclone.

Winter weather

In winter, anticyclones result in:
- cold daytime temperatures — below freezing to a maximum of 5°C;
- very cold nighttime temperatures — below freezing, with frosts;
- clear skies by day and night generally. Low level cloud may linger, and radiation fogs may remain in low-lying areas;
- high levels of atmospheric pollution in urban areas, caused by a combination of subsiding air and lack of wind. Pollutants are trapped.

Summer weather

In summer, anticyclones mean:
- hot daytime temperatures — over 25°C;
- warm nighttime temperatures — may not fall below 15°C;
- clear skies by day and night generally;
- hazy sunshine may exist in some areas;
- early morning mists/fogs will rapidly disperse;
- heavy dew on ground in the morning;
- the east coast of Britain may have sea frets/haars caused by on-shore winds;
- thunderstorms may be created when air has high relative humidity.

Features of a drainage basin system

Terminology

Base flow

That part of a river's discharge which is produced by groundwater seeping slowly into the bed of the river. It usually increases slightly during a wet spell of weather.

Interception

The process by which raindrops are prevented from falling directly on to the soil surface by the presence of a layer of vegetation. Water can be intercepted by plant leaves, stems and branches in the trees, and also by shrubs and grass. Eventually water drips off these surfaces.

Infiltration

The passage of water into the soil. Water is drawn into the soil by gravity and capillary action. It takes place at a higher rate at the start of a rainfall event, but as the soil becomes more saturated then the infiltration rate decreases.

Throughflow

The movement of water downslope within the soil. It is particularly effective where infiltration is prevented by an impermeable layer of rock. Throughflow may also take place through routeways created by tree roots and animals.

Run-off

All of the water that enters a river and flows out of the drainage basin. It is quantified by measuring the discharge of the river.

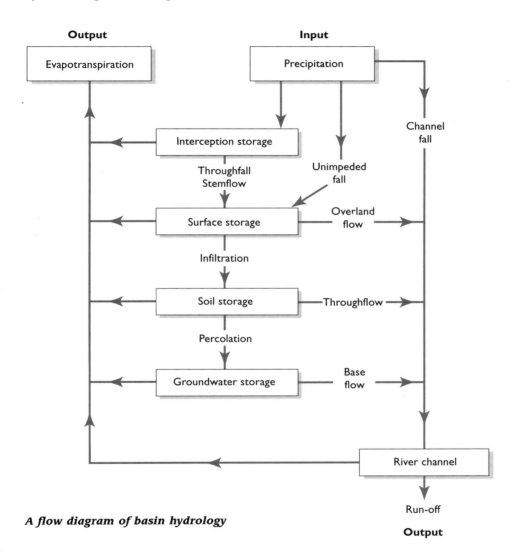

A flow diagram of basin hydrology

Storm hydrograph

A graph that shows variations in a river's discharge over a short period of time, usually during a rainstorm. The starting and finishing level shows the **base flow** of the river. As storm water enters the drainage basin the discharge rises, shown by the **rising limb**, to reach the **peak discharge**, which indicates the highest flow in the channel. The **recession limb** shows the fall in the discharge back to the base level. The time delay between maximum rainfall amount and the peak discharge is the **lag time**.

Various features influence the shape of the hydrograph:

- the intensity and duration of the storm — if both are high then they produce a steep rising limb;
- the antecedent rainfall — heavy rain falling on a soil that is saturated from a previous period of wet weather will produce a steep rising limb;
- porous soil types and/or permeable rock types produce less steep (or less flashy) hydrographs as water is regulated more slowly through the natural systems;
- a small drainage basin tends to respond more rapidly to a storm than a larger one, so the lag time is shorter;
- the influence of the vegetation in the drainage basin varies from season to season. In summer there are more leaves on the deciduous trees, so interception is higher, thus reducing peak discharge. Coniferous vegetation, planted by humans, will have less of a variable effect;
- the influence of humans in other ways can be considered. The building of roads, and the creation of hard-standing for caravan parks, creates an impermeable surface over which water runs more quickly, reducing lag time and increasing peak discharge. The grazing of cattle on the lower slopes of valleys causes trampling in some areas, which has a similar effect.

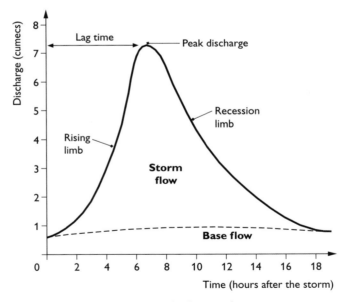

A storm hydrograph

Variations in valley long profiles and valley cross profiles of a river

Valley long profile

This shows the changes in the altitude of a river's course from its source along its channel to its mouth. In general, a long profile is smoothly concave in shape, with the gradient being steeper in the upper course and becoming progressively less steep towards the mouth. However, irregularities frequently exist, such as waterfalls, rapids and lakes.

Variations in the long profile can be explained in terms of:
- gradient — steeper in the upper part of the basin, more gentle in the lower part;
- varying rock types — resistant rocks produce waterfalls and rapids;
- natural lakes/artificial reservoirs, which flatten out the long profile;
- rejuvenation — a fall in sea level relative to the level of the land, or a rise of the land relative to the level of the sea, which revives the erosional activity of the river. The resultant steepening in the long profile is called a **knickpoint**.

Valley cross profile

This is the view of the valley from one side to another. For example, the valley cross profile of a river in an upland area has a typical V-shape, with steep sides and a narrow bottom.

Variations in the cross profile can be described and explained as follows:
- in the upper course — a narrow steep-sided valley where the river occupies all of the valley floor. This is the result of dominant vertical erosion by the river;
- in the middle course — a wider valley with distinct valley bluffs, and a flat floodplain. This is the result of lateral erosion, which widens the valley floor;
- in the lower course — a very wide, flat floodplain where the valley sides are difficult to locate. Here there is a lack of erosion and reduced competence of the river which results in large-scale deposition.

Relevant landforms that could be studied in detail include:
- waterfalls — long profile;
- knickpoints due to rejuvenation — long profile;
- floodplains and associated features (oxbow lakes, levées) — cross profile;
- river terraces — cross profile.

(a) A waterfall

(i) Origin

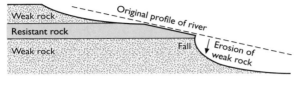

Weak rock

Original profile of river

Resistant rock

Weak rock

Fall

Erosion of weak rock

(ii) Retreat of fall

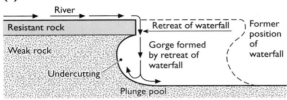

River

Resistant rock

Retreat of waterfall

Gorge formed by retreat of waterfall

Former position of waterfall

Weak rock

Undercutting

Plunge pool

(iii) Gorge created by retreat of fall

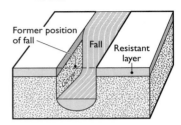

Former position of fall

Fall

Resistant layer

Gorge

(b) A meander

(i) Block diagram

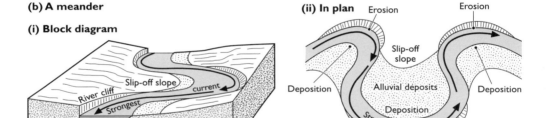

Slip-off slope

River cliff

current

Strongest

Subsurface return flow

(ii) In plan

Erosion

Erosion

Slip-off slope

Deposition

Alluvial deposits

Deposition

Deposition

Strongest river flow

Erosion

(c) The development of an oxbow lake

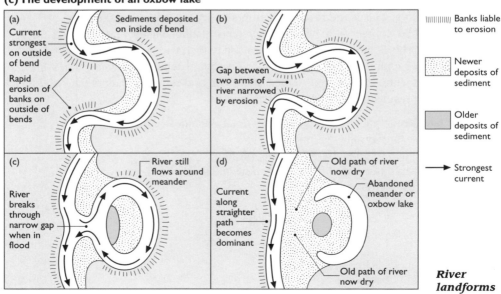

(a)
Current strongest on outside of bend

Rapid erosion of banks on outside of bends

Sediments deposited on inside of bend

(b)
Gap between two arms of river narrowed by erosion

(c)
River breaks through narrow gap when in flood

River still flows around meander

(d)
Current along straighter path becomes dominant

Old path of river now dry

Abandoned meander or oxbow lake

Old path of river now dry

Banks liable to erosion

Newer deposits of sediment

Older deposits of sediment

Strongest current

River landforms

22

(a) The upper course

(i) The generalised cross profile

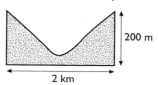

200 m

2 km

(ii) The cross profile of the River Wye 2 km southeast of the source

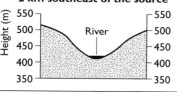

(iii) A block diagram of the typical valley

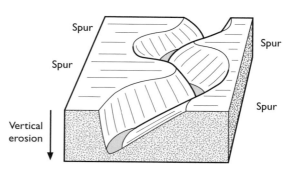

Spur

Spur

Spur

Spur

Vertical erosion

(b) The middle course

(i) The generalised cross profile

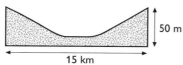

50 m

15 km

(iii) A block diagram of the typical valley

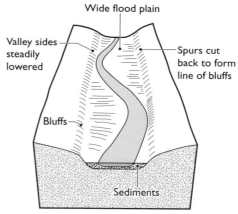

Wide flood plain

Valley sides steadily lowered

Spurs cut back to form line of bluffs

Bluffs

Sediments

(ii) The cross profile of the River Wye northeast of Hay-on-Wye

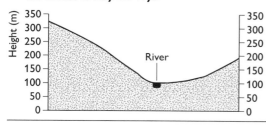

River

(c) The lower course

(i) The generalised cross profile

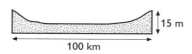

15 m

100 km

(ii) The cross profile of the River Wye south of Chepstow (mouth of the river)

River

(iii) A block diagram of the typical valley

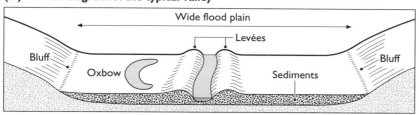

Wide flood plain

Levées

Bluff

Oxbow

Sediments

Bluff

Valley cross profile characteristics

People and the environment

Overpopulation, underpopulation and optimum population

Overpopulation

This exists when there are too many people in an area, relative to the amount of resources and the level of technology locally available, to maintain a high standard of living. It implies that, with no change in the level of technology or natural resources, a reduction in a population would result in a rise in living standards. The absolute number or density of people need not be high if the level of technology or natural resources is low.

Overpopulation is characterised by low per capita incomes, high unemployment and underemployment, and outward migration.

Underpopulation

This occurs when there are too few people in an area to use the resources efficiently for a given level of technology. In these circumstances an increase in population would mean a more effective use of resources and increased living standards for all of the people.

Underpopulation is characterised by high per capita incomes (but not maximum incomes), low unemployment, and inward migration.

Optimum population

Optimum population is defined as the theoretical population which, when working with all of the available resources, will produce the highest standard of living for the people of that area. This concept is dynamic, however, as when technology improves, new resources become available which means that more people can be supported.

Overpopulation and underpopulation refer to the imbalance in the relationship between the level of population and the use of resources. Several countries have attempted to introduce policies aimed at managing or balancing this relationship. These include:
- **social policies** of population control, for example,
  - the limiting of population growth in China (the Chinese one-child policy)
  - the encouragement of population growth in Romania in the 1980s
  - the use of immigration controls in Australia and the USA;

- **technological policies** aimed at the improvement of living standards, and levels of education, for example,
  - the use of intermediate technology in the introduction of windpumps to provide better water supplies in the Sahel countries of North Africa
  - the 'Green Revolution' — the use of high-yielding varieties of seed, with the consequent use of fertilisers, pesticides, mechanisation and irrigation
  - the development of educational improvements to increase literacy and numeracy levels in countries, which in turn attract industries to the area, as in Mauritius in the 1980s;
- **environmental policies** aimed at either increasing the amount of land that can be cultivated or improving the quality of land already available, for example,
  - land reclamation schemes in the Netherlands
  - the de-rocking scheme on the island of Mauritius, which greatly improved the quality of soils.

Optimistic and pessimistic approaches to population and resources

An optimistic approach (e.g. Ester Boserup, 1965)

Boserup, in 'The conditions of agricultural change: the economics of agrarian change under population pressure', stated that environments have limits that restrict activity. But limits can be altered by the use of appropriate technologies. Thus opportunities may be created, offering possibilities for resource development and creation. People have an underlying freedom to make a difference to their lives.

She stated that food resources are created by population pressure. In reality, farm systems become more intensive, for example by making use of shorter fallow periods. She cited certain groups of people which had reduced the fallow periods from 20 years, to periods of annual cropping, with only 2–3 months fallow, to a system of multi-cropping. Here the same plot bore 2–3 crops in the same year.

The pressure to change comes from the demand for increased food production. As the fallow period contracts, the farmer is compelled to adopt new methods and strategies to maintain yields. Thus 'necessity is the mother of invention'.

Evidence to support this approach
(1) Increasing intensity of shifting cultivation farming systems in various parts of the world from 'roca' type systems (with very low rural population densities) to systems making use of irrigation (with higher rural population densities).
(2) The widespread introduction of the 'Green Revolution' in many parts of the world. This has made use of high-yielding varieties of grains, fertilisers and pesticides, water control and mechanisation.

A pessimistic approach (e.g. Thomas Malthus, 1798 and neo-malthusians)

In 'An essay on the principle of population as it affects the future improvement of society', Malthus suggested that the environment dominates or determines patterns of human life and behaviour. Our lives are constrained by physical, economic and social factors.

His rationale was that population increases faster than the supporting food resources. If there are more children, they become parents who in turn have more children (geometric growth — 1, 2, 4, 8 etc.). Food resources cannot keep pace because they develop more slowly (arithmetic growth — 1, 2, 3, 4 etc.). The population/resource balance is maintained by various checks:
- misery — war, famine, disease;
- moral restraint — celibacy, late marriage;
- vice — abortion, infanticide, sexual perversion.

Malthus asserted that the power of a population to increase is greater than that of the earth to sustain it. This view has continued into the modern era with anxieties about the future of 'Spaceship Earth'. For example, in 1972 the Club of Rome (an international team of economists and scientists) predicted that a sudden decline in population growth could occur within a hundred years if present-day trends in population growth and resource use continued. Such people were labelled neo-malthusians. They advocated constraint, control and planning to create more stability.

Evidence to support this approach
(1) The widespread famines that have taken place in Ethiopia, Sudan and other countries of the Sahel region of Africa in recent decades, suggesting population growth has outstripped the provision of adequate food supplies.
(2) The dramatic acceleration in population growth in less economically developed countries (LEDCs) after their mortality rates began to fall. Rapid population growth is seen to impede development and to bring about a number of social and economic problems.

Two different energy systems

Biogas boilers in LEDCs (a renewable system)

This is a process by which methane gas is obtained from animal dung, human excreta and crop residues. The gas can then be used either directly as cooking fuel, or in some high-technology applications, such as fuelling high-efficiency gas turbines in order to generate electricity.

The boiler is buried in the ground. Dung and crop residues are fed into the boiler from above. An air pocket in the underground container allows methane gas to be produced, which is led off and piped to the houses or turbines. The residue and/or excess dung is used as high-quality fertiliser.

The main positive outcomes of this system are:
- a cheap source of energy;
- the safe disposal of potentially unhealthy substances.

There are also negative outcomes:
- it uses up potential sources of fuel and fertiliser, particularly those materials that also have a soil nutrient-fixing role;
- unpleasant aromas;
- it needs careful (and skilled) management to make it safe.

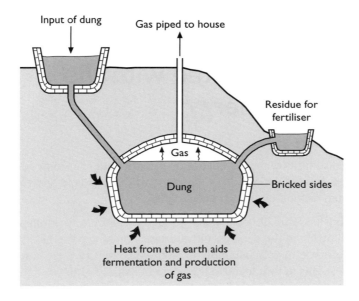

A biogas boiler

Gas-fired power stations in the UK (a non-renewable system)

The so-called 'dash for gas' in the 1990s resulted in a number of gas-fired power stations being established around the UK. The gas is pumped from the offshore fields of the North Sea. Over 30 stations have been built or are planned.

A number of factors have encouraged this:
- the development of the combined cycle gas turbine (CCGT) technology, by which more efficient use of the gas is achieved;
- gas has become more readily available, and the price of it has reduced relative to other fuels;
- the privatisation of the electricity supply industry has allowed independent companies to compete with the two main existing power station operators —

PowerGen and National Power. An example of this is the proposed CCGT station at Avonmouth, promoted by Seabank Power (a company formed by Midland Electricity and British Gas).

Gas is seen as being relatively clean and pollution-free. Modern gas-fired power stations produce very little sulphur dioxide and only a fifth of the nitrogen oxides produced by coal-fired stations. Carbon dioxide production is also 40% less than that of coal-fired stations.

One major objection to gas is that its use will be short-lived. Gas reserves in the UK may run out within 30 years, compared with proven reserves of coal for 300 years. The use of coal-fired stations has been reduced greatly, accelerating the decline of the coal industry itself. The station at Avonmouth, mentioned above, may have to supplement its gas supply by burning oil for up to 40 days a year, as 100% gas supplies are not guaranteed.

Two issues associated with the harnessing of energy

Acid deposition

Acid deposition consists of the dry deposition of sulphur dioxide, nitrogen oxides and nitric acid, and the wet deposition of sulphuric acid, nitric acid and compounds of ammonium from precipitation, mist and clouds.

Acid deposition leads to direct damage to trees, particularly coniferous trees. It produces a yellowing of the needles and strange branching patterns. It also leads to the leaching of toxic metals (aluminium) from soils, and to their accumulation in rivers and lakes. This in turn leads to the death of fish.

Acid deposition is also blamed for damage to buildings, particularly those built of limestones, and for human health problems, such as bronchitis and other respiratory complaints.

The major causes of acid deposition are the burning of fossil fuels in power stations, the smelting of metals in older industrial plants and exhaust fumes from motor vehicles.

Various solutions to acid deposition have been suggested:
- the use of catalytic converters on cars to reduce the amount of nitrogen oxides;
- burning fossil fuels with a lower sulphur content;
- replacing coal-fired power stations with nuclear power stations;
- the use of flue gas desulphurisation schemes, and other methods of removing sulphur either before coal is burned or after;
- reducing the overall demand for electricity and car travel.

Deforestation

Deforestation is the deliberate clearance of forest land by cutting or burning. It has become a major environmental concern in the LEDCs, where rainforests, such as the Amazonia region of South America, are being destroyed at an alarming rate. It is thought that half of the world's rain forests have already been destroyed, with an area the size of the UK being removed each year. By 2010 the only countries in the world with significant areas of surviving rainforest will be Brazil and Zaire.

Deforestation is taking place for the following reasons:
- the demand for hardwood (e.g. for railway sleepers, harbour piles and wharfs, solid furniture and veneering) is increasing rapidly;
- the wood is used as fuelwood, especially in parts of Africa and Asia;
- to repay the debt burdens faced by many LEDCs — for some countries the timber resources are their best way of raising capital to pay off debts;
- to exploit mineral deposits (e.g. oil, iron ore and bauxite) that lie beneath the forest floor;
- to allow the flooding of land following the construction of dams for hydroelectric power projects;
- to allow the farming of cash crops and export goods (e.g. cotton and cattle).

Consequences of deforestation include:
- the damaging effect on indigenous peoples (e.g. the Yanomani of the Amazon);
- the destruction of valuable plants as genetic resources for the future;
- the destruction of the biodiversity of the environment — plants and animals.

The hazard of nuclear waste and its management

Nuclear waste consists of both high-level and low-level radioactive material.

Nuclear power stations produce **high-level waste** consisting of used fuel rods which have been removed from the reactor. These are taken to the nuclear reprocessing plant at Thorp in Cumbria. Here reusable uranium and plutonium are separated out to leave unusable radioactive waste. This is currently placed in steel-clad glass containers which are stored nearby at Windscale.

Low-level waste includes clothing and other materials used in hospitals where exposure to radium and X-rays can present a slight risk. These materials are disposed of in controlled chemical and radiation dumps, and may also be buried in areas with suitable conditions.

In the UK, the company NIREX has been charged with the responsibility of disposing of all forms of nuclear waste, some of which does not originate in this country. It has tried (unsuccessfully so far) to find an adequate number of suitable sites for the disposal of both high-level and low-level waste.

Its most difficult task has been to find a site for the disposal of high-level waste. When examining the potential of a site for such disposal it has considered the following factors:

- the geology of the area — the ground must be geologically stable;
- the unemployment figures of the area — jobs will be created by the activity;
- the availability of land, which has to be bought for the site;
- the transport links to the site, both locally and in terms of transporting the waste long distances from nuclear power stations and ports;
- the potential strength of local pressure groups;
- the design features that will be necessary to render the site safe for many years;
- the technology that will be necessary to ensure safe transport, storage and security.

The construction of a site aimed at the safe storage of nuclear waste gives rise to a number of issues, which include:

- the noise and disruption during construction;
- short-term and longer-term safety concerns, with particular emphasis on leukaemias and cancers;
- the potential contamination of water supplies, again both in the short and longer terms;
- the effect on farming activities — will crops be safe to consume in the area, or will animals become contaminated by grazing on grass that may be affected by the waste?
- the potential risk of accidents, and the worry that the site may become a target for terrorism;
- the effect on tourism — will it destroy the tourist industry of the area, or might it actually increase its potential for visitors?
- the 'hiding and forgetting' syndrome — what future problems might arise (which are difficult to predict and plan ahead for)?
- if located in Cumbria, to what extent could the area become economically dependent on the nuclear industry?

Human geography

Manufacturing decline and growth in the UK

Manufacturing industry consists of companies that convert raw materials into finished goods or which assemble components made by other manufacturing companies. In the UK there have been a number of significant changes in the nature of manufacturing industry over the last 30 years. Some industries have undergone major decline, whereas others have grown markedly. Many of the areas of growth have been stimulated by investment from overseas.

The decline in manufacturing

There has been a general decline of the traditional heavy industries of the UK. These include:

- textiles — woollen cloth in West Yorkshire (Leeds, Bradford and Huddersfield), cotton cloth in Lancashire (Bolton, Bury and Burnley);
- steel in Sheffield and Middlesbrough;
- shipbuilding in Newcastle, Sunderland and Glasgow;
- chemicals in the northeast (Middlesbrough) and the northwest (Widnes and Runcorn);
- the car industries in the older locations, for example Birmingham and the West Midlands.

The reasons for these changes are:

- exhaustion of resources — many of the industries were originally dependent on coal, which has declined greatly in recent years;
- automation/new technology — the use of mechanisation in these industries led to job losses on a large scale;
- lack of investment — many of the traditional industries, some being owned by national government, were slow to adapt to new methodologies and money was not invested in improvements;
- alternative products/materials — some products were replaced in the global market place by cheaper, alternative products, for example plastics;
- fall in demand — the requirement for some products has fallen, for example world demand for oil tankers and other large ships fell in the 1970s and 1980s;
- overseas competition — the newly industrialised countries (NICs) of the Pacific Rim have been able to produce goods (e.g. electrical goods and textiles) at a far cheaper cost than the UK, largely due to cheaper labour costs;
- rationalisation — the reorganisation of industry to increase its overall efficiency. Many companies closed down factories and moved them to new locations,

sometimes within the UK, but often to overseas operations. In most cases, rationalisation meant redundancy;

- political factors — the widespread belief in the 1980s that British industry was inefficient and had to be modernised led to the abandonment of subsidies and other support mechanisms by national government;
- a less unionised labour force — the 'defeat' of many trades unions and the reduction in their perceived power has been a key element in the move towards greater efficiency by national government.

The growth of new manufacturing industries and new industrial areas

The majority of new manufacturing industries in the last 10–20 years have been high-technology industries, such as computers, telecommunications and micro-electronics. In addition, many of the traditional industries have advanced by adopting new technologies and working practices, for example the car assembly industry.

For these 'new' industries a highly skilled workforce is essential, and access to raw materials is less important. Consequently, such industries have become concentrated in areas where either the workforce can be attracted or is available, or the government wants to encourage them to locate.

The following are the main areas of new industrial growth:
- 'Silicon Glen' in central Scotland;
- around Cambridge and along the M11;
- the 'Sunrise Strip' of the M4 corridor;
- 'Honda Valley' in south Wales;
- the new car assembly plants in the northeast (Washington) and East Midlands (Burnaston);
- the many small, light industrial estates in 'rural areas' (e.g. East Anglia and Sussex).

The reasons for these changes are:
- inward investment by overseas transnational companies, for example by Japanese, South Korean and German firms;
- proximity to motorways/airports/high-speed rail links, for ease of communication — speed of access is important both for people and for raw materials and products;
- proximity to universities with expertise and research facilities, also enabling recruitment of highly skilled/intelligent labour (e.g. Cambridge Science Park);
- the high personal incomes of many of the above people, allowing them to establish their own businesses and to take risks;
- attractive working environments, including countryside areas or landscaped out-of-town locations. Many business and science parks have been built on greenfield sites where the relative low cost of land has also been an advantage;
- synergy — the intense, localised interaction between different firms (research organisations, banks, entrepreneurs, service organisations) on the same site, which creates benefits for all of the participants;

- aid packages from various levels of government, or from government-sponsored bodies, encouraging overseas investment to certain areas of the UK.

The growth of these new industries has allowed the **transfer of technology** to the UK. This is the movement of new working practices and other innovations into the country. These include:
- the JIT (just in time) system of production;
- worker teams rotating jobs among themselves, which helps to increase skill levels;
- the use of 'envoys' — representatives from a 'buying' industry who are permanently based in the factory of component suppliers so that they can pass on directly any required changes to design and specification;
- the use of 'milkmen' — representatives from a 'buying' industry who regularly visit the factory of component suppliers to inform them of required changes to design and specification.

Service sector growth in the UK

In the 1990s over 70% of the UK workforce was employed in the service sector. Employment in this sector can be divided into three groups: **producer services** (e.g. banks, solicitors and private distribution companies), **consumer services** (e.g. retail, hotels and leisure) and **public services** (e.g. local government, health and education).

Service sector employment has increased in all areas of the country, but concentrations tend to be more notable in:
- London — 5.5% of the UK workforce is located within central London, the vast majority of which works in service-related activity. This is one of the world's main centres for finance, business and commerce. Employment has fallen slightly in recent years, mainly as some firms have relocated to other areas in the southeast of England;
- the southeast of England — predominantly in business and finance;
- the southwest of England — largely based around tourism and the leisure industry;
- East Anglia — with significant growth in transport and communications, and in social services.

Another feature of the increase in service industries is that coastal resorts, which have traditionally provided leisure and recreation facilities, have expanded into other service activities. Bournemouth, for example, is a major conference centre out of season. It has also had a rapid expansion of its office-based employment, with the national headquarters of five companies coming to the town, including Abbey Life and Chase Manhattan.

The effects of the growth of services

The growth of the service industries has had a significant effect on employment patterns.

Gender differences

Larger numbers of females are employed, often with flexible working hours and part-time work. 'Flexitime' is now a common feature of service industry. This means that firms can respond easily and cheaply to fluctuations in demand, for example Christmas shopping at supermarkets, hotels in the summer.

Some services are becoming female-dominated — catering and hotel work are more obvious examples, but others include teaching.

More men are beginning to take on 'female roles', for example cleaning services and nursing.

Worksharing

This is a common feature in many service industries, particularly for female employees.

Homeworking and teleworking

These are increasing with the development of e-mail and video-conferencing.

Self-employment

This is increasing, both in 'low-grade' services, such as repairs and maintenance, and in 'higher-grade' services, such as insurance.

Overseas investment and its effects: an examination of attitudes

Overseas investment is the capital attracted to a region from beyond its boundaries. The UK has attracted such inward investment from a number of countries, such as Japan, South Korea, the USA and other European countries.

The main effect has been to create new industries in many areas of the UK. Some of the better known investments include car assembly plants, such as Nissan at Washington and Toyota at Burnaston. (It is expected that you will have studied one major investment in detail.)

What follows is an attempt to examine the issue of overseas investment from the perspective of the attitudes of those affected by that investment. As in any analysis of attitudes, there will be some people in favour and some people against.

Attitudes of those in favour of increased overseas investment

The investors themselves: why?

- Access to cheap, highly skilled labour
- Limited financial controls on profit
- The UK has a world currency, with a business-friendly economy
- Packages of incentives to peripheral economic areas

- Good access to EU markets
- The UK provides a quality environment, right down to the excellence of our golf courses

Governments (national and local): why?
- Inward investment of a transnational replaces the shrinking manufacturing base of a region, thus stimulating regional regeneration
- It creates a multiplier effect locally
- The export base of the country is strengthened, improving the balance of trade
- It results in effective transfer of technology and product development
- Quality standards are maintained, if not improved

Unemployed people in the area of investment: why?
- Jobs are created
- Living standards are raised

Attitudes of those against increased overseas investment

- Buccaneering transnationals may decide to leave once initial aid packages no longer apply
- Wages are said to be lower than could be the case with domestic industries
- It is costly to the taxpayer to attract the investment in the first place
- It is said that the work consists merely of screwdriver jobs, with low skill development
- Much of the employment available is part-time work
- The local area often has to bear the costs of training

Geographical segregation of social groups in urban areas of the UK

The segregation of social groups involves distinct groups of people living almost entirely separately. It produces clusters of people with similar characteristics in separate residential areas within an urban area. Examples of social segregation that have taken place in UK cities relate to personal wealth, age and ethnicity. There have been significant effects upon housing, health and education as a consequence of such segregation.

Segregation based on wealth

Many urban areas are characterised by poorer and richer people living in very different neighbourhoods. The general pattern has been one of the poor living in the inner cities and the rich living in the outer areas. This is partly to do with supply factors — small builders acquiring land tended to build housing of a similar type to that surrounding the plot, so that areas of similar housing developed. It is also due to demand factors — people usually want to live among others who share their values. Peripheral council estates with concentrations of poorer people have complicated this pattern. Similarly, the gentrification of some inner areas has inverted the original pattern. Now richer people live very near to poorer people in the inner cities, although the amount of interaction between them remains low.

The effects on housing

Areas on the edge of many cities are still mainly rich, for example Alwoodley (Leeds) and Alderley Edge (Manchester). Many inner city areas are still poor, for example Harehills (Leeds) and Collyhurst (Manchester). A lot of council house development has occurred on the edges of cities, for example Seacroft (Leeds) and Newall Green (Manchester). Furthermore, in recent years gentrification has occurred in many inner-city areas, for example the Riverside (Leeds) and Salford Quays (Manchester).

The effects on education

Schools tend to be evenly spread, due to population coverage, although higher concentrations of older Victorian schools are still located in poor inner-city areas. Out-of-town council estates have purpose-built comprehensives within them. Each new housing development tends to have its own primary school.

The quality of educational facilities varies within a town. Older schools tend to be found in poorer areas. These are often vandalised and in a poor physical state, with crumbling buildings. Private schools, and schools that have opted out of local authority control, tend to be located in more wealthy areas.

The effects on health

There is often a greater demand for health facilities in poorer areas, possibly due to a greater number of young children and elderly people. Population densities are also lower in wealthy areas, so fewer surgeries are located there.

Less affluent areas are more likely to have purpose-built facilities, in the form of health centres; in wealthy areas private houses are often converted.

Hospital location is more variable, but there is still a concentration of hospitals in the older, more central parts of a town. They are accessible to poor (public transport access) and wealthy (car access) alike. Private hospitals have a variable locational pattern. Some tend to be located in pleasant wealthy suburbs; others are located on major routeways out of town; and some are very close to the NHS provision, due to the need to share expertise and personnel.

Segregation based on age

As the number of elderly (and the age to which they live) has increased, so some degree of segregation has taken place, particularly in terms of **housing**. This has manifested itself in a number of ways.

- On council estates it is common to see clusters of purpose-built bungalows occupying one small part or parts of the estate. This has developed in some areas

into the provision of maisonettes with security access. This has followed the belief that such people are best living in the community for as long as they are fit and healthy to do so.

- A recent provision has been sheltered accommodation — a flat or unit within a larger complex with some shared facilities, overseen by a warden or manager. In some cases a mobile warden may cover a number of complexes. The location of these facilities is only just beginning to establish a pattern in some urban areas.
- Nursing homes have been increasing as the number of elderly who have difficulty looking after themselves increases. Initially, both local authorities and private developers provided such housing, but local authorities have been cutting back in their provision in recent years. In many urban areas concentrations of nursing homes are becoming clear. They are often in outer suburbs, in areas where large houses can either be converted and/or extended for this purpose.

Segregation based on ethnicity

Ethnic segregation is the clustering together of people with similar ethnic or cultural characteristics into separate residential areas within an urban area. There are numerous examples of this in the UK.

The effects on housing

In the initial phases, multiple occupancy in rented accommodation in inner-city areas (terraced houses) was widespread. The reasons were mainly to do with availability and cost. Later, more owner occupancy arose, with movements out into more suburban areas. Many immigrants run small businesses, with housing being part of the same building.

The effects on education

Concentrations of immigrants in inner-city areas have led to the domination of some schools by one ethnic group, with consequent effects on education requirements, including special English lessons for children and their parents, and bilingual reading schemes. In the more traditional parts of some cities, special religious provision is deemed necessary by the immigrant groups. This has developed into separate schooling in a minority of cases.

The effects on health

In the early phases there were problems associated with immigrant children's lack of resistance to childhood diseases, and fears over immunisation. Literature aimed at educating immigrant parents had to be produced.

As literacy standards have improved, particularly among second-generation immigrants, there have been fewer concerns. Many immigrant families and their subsequent generations continue to live in inner-city areas; these still tend to be more run down and so there remains a higher concentration of communicable and transmittable disease in such areas.

Questions
&
Answers

In this section of the guide there are six questions based on the topic areas outlined in the Content Guidance section. Each question is worth 25 marks. You should allow up to 30 minutes when attempting to answer a question, dividing that time according to mark allocation for each part. The section is structured as follows:

- sample questions in the style of the module;
- example candidate responses at the C/D grade boundary (candidate A) — these will demonstrate both strengths and weaknesses of responses with potential for improvement;
- example candidate responses at the A/B grade boundary (candidate B) — such answers demonstrate thorough knowledge, a good understanding and an ability to deal with the data that are presented in the questions. There is, however, some room for improvement. It is important to note that because of the nature of structured questions such as these, some of the sections will contain answers at the highest level, but the overall credit for the whole question will be somewhat less than that.

Examiner's comments

All candidate responses are followed by examiner's comments after each section of the answer. These examiner's comments are preceded by the icon *e*. They are inter-spersed in the answers and indicate where credit is due. In the weaker answers, they also point out areas for improvement, specific problems and common errors such as poor time management, lack of clarity, weak or non-existent development, irrelevance, misinterpretation of the question and mistaken meanings of terms.

The comments indicate how each example answer would have been marked in an actual exam. For questions with only a few available marks, examiners generally give each valid point a mark (up to the maximum possible). For higher-mark questions, examiners use a system involving 'levels':

Level I At this level, answers generally contain simple material. Points are stated briefly with no development. Examples are given in one or two words, usually in the form 'e.g....', and explanation is basic, such as 'A is the cause of B'.

Level II Answers at this level need to contain more detail. For instance, if the question requires a comparison, a Level II answer will contain some quantification, such as 'A's GDP is 10 times larger than B's'. Examples are more detailed and explanations involve clearer reasoning: 'A is the cause of B because...'.

Level III At AS there are only a few occasions when an answer is marked at Level III, usually when 9 or 10 marks are available. Marks are awarded for breadth and depth, for drawing together the threads of a response, and for overall evaluation.

Depressions and anticyclones

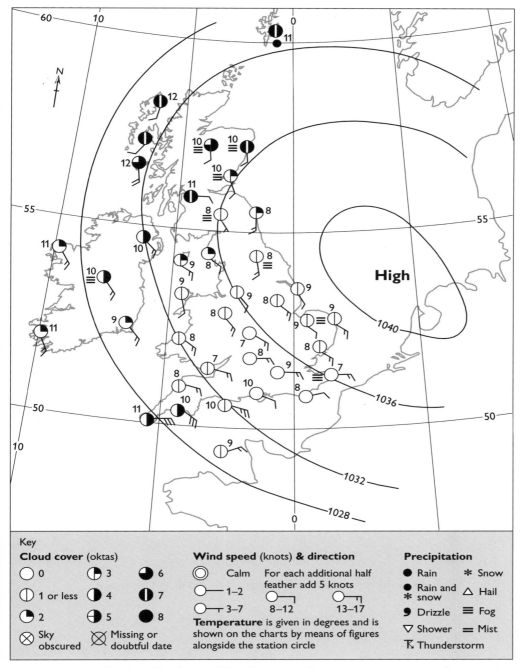

Figure 1 Synoptic chart for the British Isles, 1200 hours GMT on 28 October 1997

(a) Describe how you would measure (i) wind speed and (ii) relative humidity of the atmosphere. (4 marks)

(b) Describe the following forms of precipitation:
(i) hail
(ii) snow (4 marks)

(c) Study Figure 1 which is a synoptic chart for the British Isles at 1200 hours GMT on 28 October 1997. Compare the weather being experienced over England with that over Scotland. (6 marks)

(d) Suggest reasons for the formation of fog under anticyclonic conditions such as those shown in Figure 1. (4 marks)

(e) During the 48 hours that followed 1200 GMT on 28 October, a depression moved towards the British Isles from the Atlantic. The centre of the depression (994 mb) passed to the north of Scotland. What are the possible effects of this system on the weather experienced in the British Isles during that 48-hour period? (7 marks)

Total: 25 marks

■ ■ ■

Answer to question 1: candidate A

(a) (i) You would use an anemometer with rotating cups.
(ii) Using an instrument called a wet and dry bulb.

e In both answers the candidate has simply put forward the name of the instrument upon which the atmospheric feature can be measured. There are 4 marks available here which implies that the examiners require more than a simple statement of what is used for measuring, particularly as the question asks for a description of that measurement. An examiner would award 2 of the 4 marks for these statements.

(b) (i) Hailstones are frozen drops of water formed when raindrops freeze.
(ii) Snow occurs when atmospheric conditions are below freezing. In such circumstances snow forms instead of drops of water.

e As in section (a) these are simplistic answers, putting forward only one real point in each part. In (i) the candidate could have referred to the possible structure of hailstones, rime and glaze, or even some reference to size, while in (ii) nothing was put forward with reference to crystals. The fact that 4 marks are available suggests that the examiners are looking for two correct statements for each, although they would probably accept three points for one feature and only one for the other. The answer on snow may appear to have two points, but the second sentence only states that snow forms in those circumstances — it does not describe it.

(c) Scotland seems to be warmer than England with there generally being more cloud over Scotland. Wind speeds do not seem to be all that different, the direction in most places being south or east or somewhere in between. Scotland, though, has generally southern winds, whereas they are from the east in England. Several places in both countries are experiencing fog.

e The command word **compare** means that the answer should provide a point-by-point account of the similarities and differences between the weather of England and that of Scotland. The maximum mark of 6 at AS means that the answers will be level-marked. This is an answer that contains simple points of comparison, which could only be credited within Level I of a mark scheme. To raise this answer into the Level II area, some reference should have been made to the actual temperatures and the amount of cloud cover. Wind speed and direction is not as simplistic as is made out in this answer and there should have been reference to this point. Finally, there are large areas of England where there is no fog. The candidate is correct in observing fog in both countries, but a better answer would have gone further. Overall, it is clear that the candidate has some idea of how to read a meteorological map, but the material presented is directed at too simple a level.

(d) The fog that has formed under such anticyclonic conditions is known as radiation fog. As there are no clouds to hold in the heat produced by day, the heat radiates into space at night and as the air cools, fog is formed. This can sometimes last all day, as is shown on the weather map, i.e. 12 noon.

e The candidate knows something about the formation of such fog but too many points are simply stated without any real knowledge being shown with regard to formation — 'the air cools, fog is formed...this can sometimes last all day'. For higher marks these links would have to be explained. This answer would receive 2 of the maximum 4 marks for the section. Given the position of the anticyclone and the wind off a cool North Sea, the examiners would have accepted an answer on advection fog had it been given.

(e) The depression coming from the Atlantic will bring its fronts and these will spread cloud and rain across the British Isles. Also the wind will increase as depressions have stronger winds than anticyclones. The wind direction will be from the Atlantic side as the depression moves in from that direction.

e As with previous answers, the candidate shows some understanding of weather systems but not the detail necessary for marks at the highest level. All that is being said is that it will become windier, cloudier and wetter. The answer completely ignores the variations in weather that a depression can bring and also does not consider the possible scenario of the 'blocking anticyclone'. This answer would receive 3 of the maximum 7 marks.

■ ■ ■

Answer to question 1: candidate B

(a) (i) Wind speed is measured by an anemometer where the wind sends round the rotating cups of the instrument and the measurement is made by counting, or reading from a digital counter, the number of revolutions in a given time. Revolutions can be converted into metres per second by using a calibration chart.

(ii) The wet and dry bulb thermometer consists of two thermometers, one of which is covered in a damp cloth (the wet bulb). You read the dry bulb, find how many degrees the wet bulb is below it and compare your results with a chart that will give the relative humidity. This is always expressed as a percentage of the water vapour that it could be holding.

e These are good answers as they both describe the instrument and how it is actually used to measure the atmospheric feature. More detail could have been given in the last sentence with some reference to temperature, but given that only 4 marks are available here, this answer comfortably qualifies for that mark.

(b) (i) Raindrops are carried up into higher sections of clouds where they freeze. Layers of ice form upon them which are opaque (called rime). When they fall the outer sections may melt and then refreeze to form a glazed layer which gives the hailstone its banded appearance. They fall as showers when they become heavy enough.

(ii) Snow is when ice crystals aggregate to form a larger unit, a snowflake. They form when temperatures are below zero and vapour forms straight away into a solid rather than a water droplet.

e Both these answers carry far more detail than those given by candidate A. Part (i) would certainly receive 3 of the 4 mark maximum for the question. Better answers may mix up description with some elements of the formation of the feature, but it is not always easy to split them when assessing the answer. Almost all of what has been written above could be taken for description.

(c) Scotland is warmer than England with 8–12 °C against 7–11. Wind speeds are very similar generally between 15 and 20 knots, with the direction usually coming from the east or south. There is very little cloud cover over England, whereas there is more over Scotland. Nowhere has complete cloud cover.

e Some comparisons are made, but the picture presented seems too general and lacks detailed observation. The temperature over Scotland for most of the country is 10–12 °C, whereas over England it is mainly 7–9°C. Some reference could have been made to the higher temperatures and cloud cover over southwest England and to the wind directions which are not as simplistic as made out in the answer.

(d) Under anticyclonic conditions the lack of cloud cover allows heat to radiate away into space and the air close to the ground to cool rapidly. If it drops below its dew point the air will condense to produce fog which is called radiation fog. There are also light winds which mean that the fog will not be blown away and may persist for a long time.

e This answer does enough to qualify for all the marks, although there are areas where it could be improved. It is not the air which condenses, it is the water vapour within it which produces the fog's tiny droplets. Although the last sentence is partly correct, it is the inability of the sun to break through the fog and warm the lower atmosphere in order to produce evaporation which also allows the fog to persist.

(e) As the depression moves in, the warm front will cross the British Isles and produce some rainfall, as will the cold front which follows it. Therefore the weather will become much cloudier and it will become warmer as the wind comes in from the west rather than from the east as shown on the map. Depressions will also spread windier conditions across Britain.

e This answer will access **Level II** of the mark scheme as it includes some detail of the passage of a depression, although the answer could be improved to reach the higher marks. **Reference** could be made to the passage of the warm sector followed by the cold, the showery pattern of the cold sector and the reason for the stronger winds. Some reference could also be made to the fact that the anticyclone may not give way and act as a 'blocking' feature which will mean that the full sequence of the passage of a depression is not likely to be experienced.

Basin hydrology

(a) In the context of basin hydrology, what is meant by
   (i) interception and (ii) base flow?   (4 marks)

(b) You have undertaken fieldwork involving the collection of data. (For example,
   in the study of a drainage basin you may have had to sample locations at which
   to measure rates of infiltration.) Describe a method of data collection which you
   used in your fieldwork.   (5 marks)

(c) Compare the storm hydrographs for the stations P, Q and R (Figure 2) as shown
   on Figure 1.   (8 marks)

(d) Suggest reasons for any differences that you have observed between hydrographs
   P, Q and R.   (8 marks)

Total: 25 marks

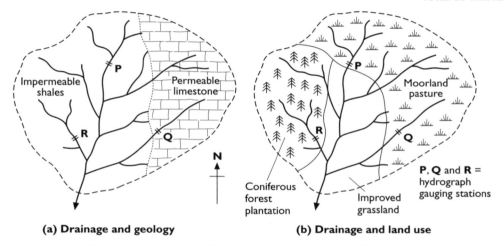

(a) Drainage and geology   (b) Drainage and land use

Figure 1 An upland drainage basin in the British Isles

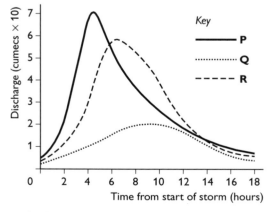

Figure 2 Storm hydrographs for each of gauging stations P, Q and R

■ ■ ■

Answer to question 2: candidate A

(a) (i) Interception is when vegetation stops raindrops.

(ii) Base flow is what keeps a river flowing when there is no rain.

e As 4 marks are available here, examiners are expecting more than two simple statements. These statements are correct but would only receive 1 mark each. The greater detail given by candidate B below receives the other 2 marks.

(b) I would choose my locations at which to measure rates of infiltration by using a random method of sampling. This is easy to use as it involves simply selecting a number of points on a map using a random method such as a pin or a pencil point (with your eyes closed).

e This would gain Level I marks as the candidate names the method and puts forward a very simple way in which it can be used. Nothing is specifically presented that relates to the task undertaken, which would qualify for Level II marks. On this particular question, the candidate can use any piece of fieldwork that has involved the collection of data. This example has taken the topic from the study suggested in the question wording.

(c) All the three hydrographs start from the same place although they all have different lag times, that for station Q being very much behind the others. The maximum discharge is also different in all three although they all finish roughly at the same point. This means that they all have different shapes.

e This answer compares the three hydrographs, as required in the question, but does so in rather a simplistic way. The candidate does recognise lag time but only says that each station is different and fails to indicate how they are different. The same is true for maximum discharge (although reference should have been made to 'peak') and also for the amount of water that is actually discharged. Although the candidate has covered a number of features, they are so simplistically put that only credit within Level I of a mark scheme would be awarded.

(d) Station P is situated on impermeable shales and in an area of moorland pasture which means that there is very little to stop the water reaching the river and this explains the lag time and the large maximum discharge. Station R is also situated on the impermeable rock but is covered with coniferous forest which slows down the water and alters the hydrograph with a lower maximum discharge and a longer lag time. Station Q is on a different rock type, permeable limestone, which means that water is able to soak in and not go down to the river. Although the moorland pasture is less than the coniferous forest in stopping the water, the storm hydrograph is very much less than the other two.

e All that has been written is correct (although water does not soak through limestone, it passes down joints, etc.) but the links between the features of the drainage basin and the storm hydrograph are not made clear. This answer would therefore only be awarded credit within Level I of a mark scheme because although the differences in rock type and vegetation are somewhat developed, the material does not go on to show the effects that they have on the movement of water within the drainage basin.

■ ■ ■

Answer to question 2: candidate B

(a) (i) Interception is the process by which raindrops are prevented from falling directly on to a soil surface by vegetation. Water can be intercepted by the leaves and branches of trees and grass and shrubs.

(ii) Base flow is the water coming from the ground either side of the river which keeps it flowing even when it is not raining. Without it the river would dry up.

e This would achieve the maximum mark of 4, although the answer to the first part is much better than that to part (ii). In the section on base flow, reference could have been made to groundwater flow and to the fact that base flow tends to be fairly constant in rivers that flow all year.

(b) When I was investigating shopping habits (for both high and low order goods) in a village in a study of catchment areas, I decided to carry out a 10% sample in the village which meant sampling 10% of the houses, as I intended to carry out a doorstep survey. The method I chose was a systematic sample which meant that I devised a route through the village that would take me past every house and I would ask questions at the tenth, the twentieth, the thirtieth and so on, therefore there was a distinct pattern to the survey. This removed any bias that could have occurred. If the inhabitants were not in, I arranged to go back and to interview them at a different time.

e This is a good answer as it identifies the form of data collection used and links it to the actual study. The candidate also includes detail and justifies the use of the method in that it should remove bias from the sample. Although the whole of this question is physically based, it is possible in such a section on fieldwork for the survey to be drawn from any part of the candidate's geographical work.

(c) In terms of the lag time, the hydrograph at station P shows that there is a quicker response time than for both stations R and Q, which is particularly slow as compared to P. This means that the rising limb (the one on the left) is steeper in P and R than in Q with a corresponding angle on the falling limb. The peak discharge of station P is large along with that for station R which is not far behind. Station Q's peak discharge is considerably below that of the other two. It is noticeable that all the hydrographs start and finish at roughly the same place on the graph. The hydrographs for P and R are also considerably bigger in size than that for station Q.

e Comparisons are clearly made here, as is requested by the wording of the question, and such material can be awarded credit within Level II of a mark scheme. The main thing lacking within the answer, however, is some form of quantification. The hydrograph is set within the context of a graph, so it is possible to say to what extent the lag times and peak discharges vary. Reference could have also been made to the amount of water being discharged past each point rather than one hydrograph being seen as bigger than the other. This answer would not be credited with the higher marks of Level II.

(d) The lag time for each of the stations is different because of the different rock upon which they stand. Those stations on the impermeable rock have a quicker response time as water does not soak in and gets to the river faster, whereas the station on the limestone has water which passes down through the rock and does not reach the river. This means that the river responds slower than the first two.

There are two stations on the moorland pasture which means that rainwater is not well intercepted and should reach the river quickly, which is the case for station P, but Q is also on a permeable rock which allows much of the water to go underground. Trees will intercept more of the rainwater with their leaves and branches which is why station R has a slower lag time and peak discharge than station P. Overall, stations P and R have a greater discharge than Q because they lie on impermeable rock, so more of the rain water will get down to the river.

e There are some good points in this answer which enable the examiners to give credit at Level II. The candidate recognises the importance of vegetation and rock type in developing differences in the storm hydrographs, but the movements of water inside the drainage basin are still not fully detailed. For maximum credit the candidate should have explained how vegetation and rock type contribute not only to interception and infiltration but also to overland flow and throughflow (P vs Q) and interception/infiltration/evapotranspiration (P vs R).

Population

(a) **Study Figure 1. Compare the rate of increase in the world population with the rates of increase in the regions shown.** (4 marks)

(b) **The information in Figure 1 is displayed on a logarithmic scale. What are the advantages and disadvantages of using this method for such material?** (4 marks)

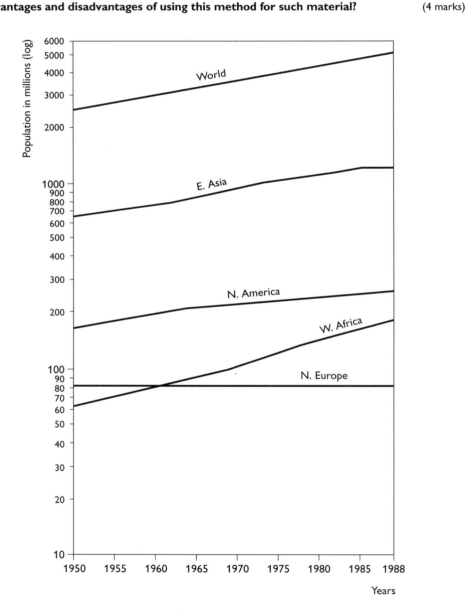

Figure 1 World population growth by region, 1950–1988

(c) Study Figure 2. (i) Describe the world distribution of infant mortality rates.
(ii) Comment on the relationship between the distribution of infant mortality
rates (Figure 2) and world population growth by regions (Figure 1). *(8 marks)*

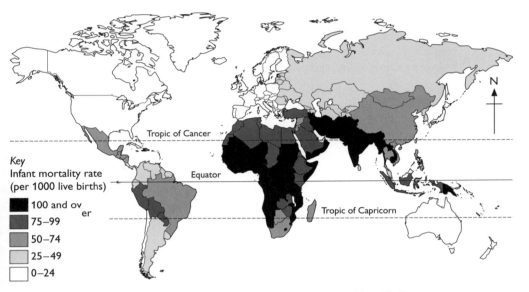

Figure 2 World infant mortality rates per 1000 live births, 1990

(d) Many countries have developed policies to try to solve the problems which have
arisen as a consequence of their population growth rates. With reference to
examples, describe the nature of three different policies and show how successful
they have been. *(9 marks)*

Total: 25 marks

■ ■ ■

Answer to question 3: candidate A

(a) The world population has shown a steady rise between 1950 and 1988, rising from
about 2000 million to 5000 million. East Asia rose steadily and then flattened off
from around 1985. North America's rise slowed down after 1965, rising from under
200 million to just over. West Africa has increased at roughly the same rate for the
whole period. North Europe has steadily gone down since 1950, starting above 80
million and finishing in 1988 below it.

🖉 Whilst the candidate has been able to interpret the logarithmic graph correctly, the
answer consists of simple statements and does not carry out the comparison
required by the question wording. As all the statements are correct, the examiners
would award 2 of the maximum 4 marks for this answer. Examiners in such circumstances are looking for comparative words such as 'faster', 'greater', 'slower', 'more
than double the rate in', and they will also accept statements linked by such words

as 'whereas'. Anything else, as with this answer, is expecting the examiner to carry out the work that should have been done by the candidate.

(b) Logarithmic graphs can show how things change through time and you can compare different rates of change. They are difficult to read and to plot.

e The statements here are too simplistic to be rewarded with anything but modest credit. It is true that you can compare different rates of change, but the candidate has not said how this is accomplished.

(c) (i) Infant mortality rates are highest in the Developing World, particularly in Africa and parts of southern Asia. They are lowest in North America, Europe, Australia and parts of South America. There seems to be a definite difference between the Developed and Developing Worlds.

(ii) The population of East Asia is steadily increasing and the infant mortality rates seem to be high and this is the same for West Africa where the rates are the highest in the world. In North America the rate of infant mortality is low and the population is increasing. In North Europe the infant mortality rate is low but the population is decreasing.

e All the statements made in the two sections are correct but the observations made by the candidate would confine the credit awarded to within Level I of a mark scheme. In part (i) the map has been correctly read and the candidate has noted the major variations that can be seen, but there is nothing on regional variations or on any anomalies that exist. In part (ii) the material consists of a straightforward comparison between the two sets of data, nothing being put forward on the rate of population change in comparison to Figure 2.

(d) There are many different policies to try to solve these problems. In China they have a policy of only allowing families to have one child, known as the One Child Policy. This is a complete change from the past in China when families had many children. It has not been a success in some areas as people with a history of large families resent being told what to do by the state.

Many countries, such as India and Bangladesh, have had policies of birth control where people are issued with such things as condoms and pills for women to take and they are educated as to how to use them. The trouble in such countries is that people do not always understand what they are doing and they need many children to work in the fields to replace those who die because of the high infant mortality rate. That is why they have not been all that successful with these programmes.

Some countries have tried to control migration into their countries as a way of stopping population growing. In Britain recently the government has decided to become tougher on asylum seekers who come from many parts of the world. This policy has not really worked as it is difficult to stop many of these people as they come here illegally.

e The candidate has covered three policies as requested and they do cover different approaches to the situation. There is, however, little detail in describing the nature of the policies and the candidate is not really aware of the actual policies of the governments of India and Bangladesh which are quoted in the answer. Britain is said to have tougher immigration policies, but they have not been identified within the answer. There is an attempt in each case to state the success of these policies but again this is put in only the simplest of terms, although the candidate will receive some credit for attempting to say what the problems have been. All the comments on success are put in a negative way. The candidate could also have covered policies that increase resources, such as the Green Revolution, as the question does not confine candidates to dealing with only policies on population.

■ ■ ■

Answer to question 3: candidate B

(a) The world population shows a steady rise from about 2500 million to 5000 million. East Asia rises at a comparable rate but the rate of increase decreases slightly about 1970 and again in 1985. North America shows a broadly similar rise to around 1965 and then reduces to a slower rate. West Africa has a constant rate but its growth is at a much higher rate than the world population. North Europe is completely different, showing no population growth and probably a slight decrease.

> 🖉 This is a good answer because the candidate is doing exactly what is asked in the question, comparing the world population growth rate with that of the regions. Statements such as 'the rate of increase decreases slightly' shows that this candidate has a complete understanding of the material. The maximum mark would be awarded.

(b) The advantage in showing such figures is that logarithmic scales are useful when the rate of change is being examined. A steeper line reveals a faster rate of change and vice versa. Logarithmic graphs can also allow a wider range of data to be displayed than you can on ordinary graph paper. This is important here as the numbers range from 10 million to 6000 million. The main drawback to such graphs is that it is not possible to plot zero, so the base line is always a positive number and this could confuse some people if they were not aware of what they were reading.

> 🖉 The candidate has made a number of good points here about logarithmic scales and has also related them to the population growth material presented in Figure 1. Such an answer would receive the maximum marks for this section.

(c) (i) Infant mortality rates are generally much higher in the Developing World than in the Developed. High rates are seen through Africa and southeast Asia, particularly in the Indian subcontinent, and in parts of South America. Low rates are seen through North America, Europe, Japan and Australia/New Zealand. Not all Africa is in the highest category.

(ii) The faster the rate of population increase as seen in Figure 1, the higher the infant mortality rate in Figure 2. West Africa seems to be rising fastest by the end of the graph and most of the area is in the highest category for infant mortality. North America and Northern Europe, which have seen the smallest rate of increase (perhaps even a decrease in Europe), have the lowest levels of infant mortality seen.

e There are several good points within both sections of this answer. In part (i) the candidate has not only seen the general pattern but made specific place references within it. The answer also attempts to pick out any regional variations, although it could have gone further as there are a number of anomalies present on the map (Sri Lanka, for example). The link between Figures 1 and 2 has been established in this answer, although the material would be improved by some attempt to comment on why the two variables appear to be linked, i.e. why a low rate of increase should equate with a low infant mortality. This answer would be marked well inside Level II, but would not be marked at the very highest level.

(d) There are many different types of scheme which are trying to solve the problems of large population growths. Some schemes have been trying to help people to help themselves by providing such things as condoms and birth pills within the framework of a birth control programme. Here people are persuaded of the need to limit births by an education programme such as that run by the government of Sri Lanka. This policy has been reasonably successful in reducing the birth rate of the country, but there was opposition on moral grounds and by the leaders of the two communities in the country as they were frightened that one group might then outbreed the other.

In China there is a forced policy called the One Child Policy. In this the Chinese are restricted to one child per family in order to reduce population growth below replacement level. This has been running for a number of years and will continue well into the twenty-first century. It has been successful in urban China but in rural parts farmers still want to have a son to run their farms when they get old and to look after them.

Some countries have viewed the problem from a different aspect in that they have focused their attention on trying to provide more resources to deal with the increasing population numbers. A good example of such schemes is provided by the Green Revolution which has attempted to get farmers to produce more from existing land by using high yielding varieties of crops. In some areas, however, only the richer farmers have gained benefits from the scheme as poorer farmers have found that they require enormous amounts of fertilisers to make these new crops grow.

e There is some good material in this answer which would certainly receive credit within Level II of a mark scheme, but there are areas where the material could be improved. As the candidate will have studied population policies, at the higher level an examiner could expect quantitative details to be included. It is encouraging to see in this answer that the candidate has looked beyond policies that are designed simply to limit population growth, although at this level one might expect a more direct reference to where this scheme was in place and the level of success that had occurred. Policies could also be considered where population growth rates are low and countries are encouraging immigration.

Energy

(a) Study Figures 1 and 2.

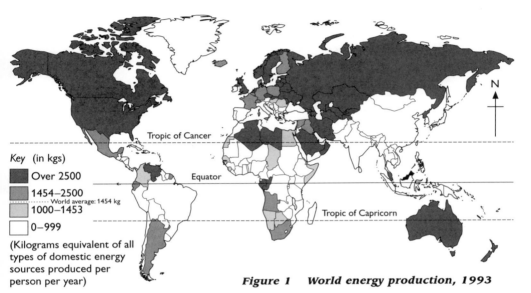

Key (in kgs)

■ Over 2500

▨ 1454–2500
-------- World average: 1454 kg
▨ 1000–1453

□ 0–999

(Kilograms equivalent of all types of domestic energy sources produced per person per year)

Figure 1   World energy production, 1993

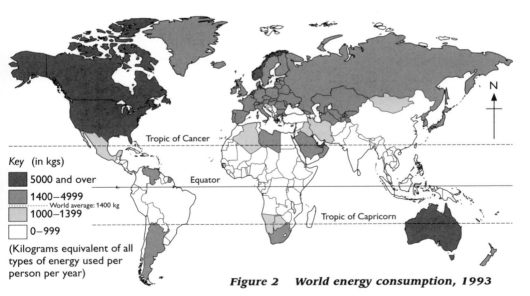

Key (in kgs)

■ 5000 and over

▨ 1400–4999
-------- World average: 1400 kg
▨ 1000–1399

□ 0–999

(Kilograms equivalent of all types of energy used per person per year)

Figure 2   World energy consumption, 1993

(i) **Describe the world distribution of energy production (Figure 1).**   (4 marks)

(ii) **Compare the world distribution of energy production with that of energy consumption (Figure 2).**   (4 marks)

4

question

(b) **Describe the advantages and disadvantages of the choropleth technique used to display the information shown in Figures 1 and 2.** (4 marks)

(c) **With reference to a country that you have studied:**

   (i) **Describe the proportions of the different sources of energy used and suggest reasons for this pattern.** (7 marks)

   (ii) **Outline the environmental damage that could result from using the sources of energy that you have described in (i).** (6 marks)

Total: 25 marks

■ ■ ■

Answer to question 4: candidate A

(a) (i) There is a high level of energy production in North America, the former USSR, some parts of Europe such as Britain, in North Africa and the Middle East and Australia. Low levels of production are seen in South America, most of Africa and southeast Asia.

   e This is a straightforward account that simply lists most of the areas that fall into either the high or low categories. No wider categories are looked at along with any anomalous areas that might exist within those patterns. Such material would receive 2 of the 4 marks available here.

   (ii) Areas of high production and consumption are seen in North America, parts of Europe and Australia. Low levels of production and consumption occur in most of South America, southeast Europe, central Africa and southeast Asia. Some areas produce a lot and do not consume much, such as parts of Africa, and some are the other way around.

   e The bulk of the statements here are of the high/high and low/low variety with only a short reference to high/low and low/high. In addition, the candidate has only concentrated on the highest and lowest categories in the key. High, for example, is only considered where the shading is at its darkest, making it difficult to find areas of low production/high consumption, of which Japan is a good example (Japan is not in the highest category for consumption).

(b) The choropleth technique is a shading map which, because dark colours represent a high category and light colours a low one, is easy to read and to see the information that is being presented. A drawback with this approach is that huge areas are often covered by the same shading when there could be some variety within them.

   e Two good points are raised here, one advantage and one disadvantage, which would receive 2 of the 4 marks available. The answer concentrates on reading the maps, nothing being put forward from the point of view of the person using the technique.

(c) (i) In Britain we use a range of different sources of energy. Coal was once the major form of energy used but this has now declined to only a fraction, as most coal mines have been closed down and we now generate electricity by other means.

Recently the government has allowed the building of more gas-fired power stations using the natural gas from the North Sea, as this is a cheaper way to produce electricity. Britain also has huge oil deposits under the North Sea, which we use mainly as petrol for cars and for our petrochemical industry.

Britain was one of the first countries to use nuclear power and there are a large number of stations operating in Britain, such as Sellafield.

We also use hydroelectric power (HEP), although not as much as other countries such as Switzerland and Norway. In Britain there are a number of places where wind is used to generate electricity and we are experimenting with such things as tidal power, which has been suggested for the Severn estuary.

e The candidate has some idea of the energy base of Britain but really fails to describe the proportions used, as requested by the wording of the question. This means that the mark received can only be within Level I, as the answer is coupled with only fairly sketchy attempts at reasoning. Credit would be given for some of the locational material, but this candidate (like many candidates) could not think of a nuclear power station and so named Sellafield (which is a nuclear reprocessing plant)! It is probably the only name that many candidates remember as being associated with the nuclear industry.

(ii) Coal burning puts gases into the atmosphere which produce acid rain and lead to global warming. Such gases may also be responsible for damage to the ozone layer which will bring about more cases of skin cancer. The same could be said for burning oil and gas, but not to the same extent. The hazards of nuclear power are well known, especially after the explosion of Chernobyl in Russia which caused a lot of contamination in Britain, particularly in upland areas such as the Lake District, and affected sheep. Oil is often transported by tanker, and when these run aground, huge oil spills occur which contaminate beaches and wildlife.

e Even with the use of the command word 'outline', the examiners could have expected more detail within the answer. For example, it should have been possible to refer to carbon dioxide and to some of the effects of global warming. The material on nuclear power is again fairly vague in that it refers to contamination and that it 'affected sheep'. The answer would also have benefited from a greater use of examples. A mistake that is seen repeatedly in answers at this level is that coal burning, and the gases that it produces, is responsible for damage to the ozone layer.

■ ■ ■

Answer to question 4: candidate B

(a) (i) It seems that a lot of the more developed countries (MEDCs) produce large amounts of energy, e.g. USA, Canada, UK, Norway, Russia, Australia. Many of the poorer countries (LEDCs) produce low levels of energy, as can be seen in South America, over much of Africa and southeast Asia. Such countries are Brazil, India and China. The pattern, though, is not that simple, as some countries in Europe produce low levels whilst there are a number of countries in Africa, particularly the north, and in the Middle East which produce large amounts.

> *e* This is a good answer, showing that the candidate has a clear grasp of the pattern which is seen not to be as simple as high energy production equating with high levels of development.

(ii) High levels of production of energy and high levels of consumption are seen in Canada, USA, parts of northern Europe (including Britain and Norway), Russia and Australia, which are all developed countries (MEDCs), and in parts of the Middle East and northern parts of Africa which are LEDCs. Low production levels go together with low consumption levels in much of South America, Africa and southeast Asia (including India and China). There are several examples of countries having high production but low consumption and these will be LEDCs which do not need the energy but probably export it. Examples come from Africa and the Middle East, such as Saudi Arabia. There are also examples of MEDCs that do not produce much in the way of energy but which need it in their economies, e.g. Japan, Spain.

> *e* This is almost the complete answer and probably is too long for a 4 mark question. The material, however, covers all the major points as the candidate has tried to find examples of the four categories that can be extracted from such 'eyeball' correlation exercises. These are high/high and low/low together with high/low and low/high and an examination of them will always produce a high-scoring answer where only a straightforward comparison is required without any reasoning.

(b) Choropleth maps are easy to read as they show high and low areas very well by using the density of shading, as dark areas clearly indicate high figures. Drawbacks are that one type of shading often covers wide areas where there may be some variation and that you have to make abrupt boundaries where one type of shading gives way to another and this sudden change may not exist in reality.

> *e* The candidate has made some good observations but was weakest on the advantages of using the system. Other points that could be considered include the advantage of showing spatial distributions and the fact that actual numbers cannot be used, as figures have to be grouped into classes. This answer would be awarded 3 of the 4 marks available.

(c) (i) In the 1990s Japan's major source of energy was oil which accounted for over 50% of all energy used, although only a small percentage of electricity was produced using that fuel, most oil going as petrol for cars. This was surprising as Japan has to import nearly all its oil as it has very little of its own. It does have some coal which it mines and it also imports from other parts of the world, and Japan relies for about 20% of its energy on coal. Natural gas and nuclear energy have been increasing in recent years as Japan is a high technology country and, being rich, can also pay for the technology that it needs. There is some HEP from the Japanese mountain areas and geothermal, as Japan is volcanic. The main forms above account for almost all Japan's energy usage.

e This is a Level II answer as the candidate does show knowledge of some details of the energy usage of the chosen country of Japan. The question asks for the proportions of the different sources and the candidate has given that information for coal and oil but not, unfortunately, for the others. Some are said to be 'increasing' and others are simply stated as 'some'. Examiners would expect far more detail if they were to consider an answer worth higher marks in Level II. The answer could also have been improved by more details within the reasoning part. The candidate has put some reasoning forward for most of the sources, but at this level one expects more information than that Japan is mountainous and volcanic. Although this will attract some credit, it will not put the answer into the highest mark area.

(ii) Coal burning produces carbon dioxide which is a greenhouse gas, the build up of which is said to be responsible for global warming. It also puts sulphur in the atmosphere resulting in acid rain which damages trees and buildings. The same can be said for oil which is responsible for pollution in cities as a result of car exhaust fumes. Oil tankers often run aground and cause oil slicks and the crude oil gets onto beaches and rocks. The hazard of nuclear power is well known following the accident at Chernobyl in Russia where a nuclear power station blew up and contaminated much of Russia and Europe, including Britain where sheep got high doses of radiation fall-out. There have also been problems in America such as that at the Five-Mile Island nuclear plant.

e Several good points are made within this answer, although some of the material is simplistic and would improve with more accurate and detailed information (the material on nuclear power, for example). More detail could be expected on global warming and nothing was written on nuclear waste. Other forms of environmental damage could have been included as some environmentalists consider that HEP schemes can be damaging. There is also the argument for visual pollution that can be put forward. This answer would certainly qualify for over half of the 6 marks available but it would not be credited at the very highest level.

Question 5

Manufacturing in the UK

(a) Describe the regional variations in new manufacturing jobs created by overseas investment within the UK between 1979 and 1993, as shown in Figure 1. In your answer you should refer to both the numbers of jobs created and their relative importance. (5 marks)

(b) Suggest reasons why foreign companies, when considering investment in the UK, find some areas more attractive than others. (5 marks)

(c) (i) Identify the geographical areas in the UK where employment in the service sector is increasing. (3 marks)

(ii) Suggest two reasons for the growth in the service sector. (4 marks)

(d) Suggest another way in which one of the two pieces of information shown in Figure 1 could be represented and explain how you would carry out the technique. (4 marks)

(e) Explain the growth in homeworking that has taken place in recent years. (4 marks)

Total 25: marks

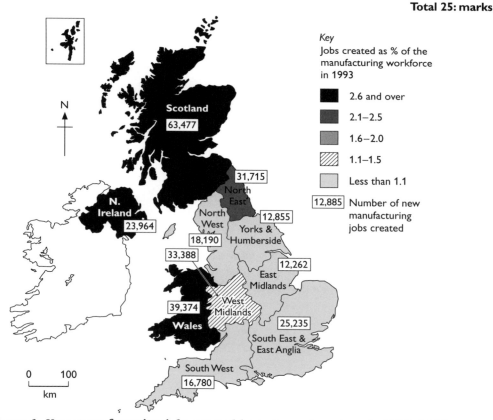

Figure 1 New manufacturing jobs created by overseas investment, 1979–1993

Answer to question 5: candidate A

(a) The largest percentage of jobs created by foreign investment is to be found in Scotland, N. Ireland and Wales. The lowest levels in percentage terms are through most of England. Scotland saw the largest number of jobs created from this investment at 63,477 followed by Wales at 39,374 and then the West Midlands at 33,388. Some of the eastern areas have created the smallest number of jobs, namely the East Midlands with 12,262 and Yorkshire and Humberside with 12,855. The southwest and northwest were also low. In the main, the 'North' seems to have attracted more jobs than the 'South'.

> ✒ This is a typical Level I answer in that the candidate has done little more than lift the information from Figure 1 and do nothing with it. There is an attempt in the last sentence to try to see some overall pattern.

(b) Many foreign firms are attracted to one region rather than another because they may find a workforce there which suits their particular industry. Sites may also be available at the right price which may be far more expensive elsewhere. There may also be financial incentives offered by the government if they will go to a certain region.

> ✒ As with part (a), this is another fairly simplistic answer which could only expect credit at Level I in a mark scheme or 2 or 3 marks on a point marking system. At this level, details are expected on the type of workforces that firms could be looking for and of incentive packages that could also be offered by the regional or local authorities. Other factors that could be mentioned include the quality of the environment and the infrastructure of the region concerned.

(c) (i) The service sector has been growing in the 'South' in areas such as southeast England and East Anglia. It has also been growing in most of the major urban centres of the UK, such as London, Birmingham and Manchester.

> ✒ Of a 3 mark maximum here, the candidate could expect 2 marks for this answer. The service sector has been growing over the whole of the UK, as it is a national phenomenon. The candidate has correctly identified the key areas, although some authorities would say that it is only central London and not the city as a whole which has seen developments in the service sector.

(ii) There has been a decline in the manufacturing sector in the UK which has led to a growth in service areas. The introduction of technology has increased employment in such areas as the Internet and mobile phones. Another feature has been the growth of financial services, particularly Internet banking.

> ✒ The candidate has some idea but there is very little here to suggest reasons for this growth. A decline in one area, manufacturing, does not necessarily mean an increase in another, services. The candidate knows what constitutes services but has thrown in anything he/she can think of as being connected with it, such as mobile phones and the Internet. How many jobs in traditional banking has Internet

banking destroyed? Has it led to a growth in the service sector or a decline? Of the 4 marks available, this answer would be awarded credit very much at the lower end.

(d) Taking the information of the percentage of the workforce, you could put the information on a bar chart. First of all you would need to get the exact percentages for such regions and then plot them on a bar chart which is done on graph paper. You need to decide a scale and then plot each region on the chart with a bar which is proportional in length to the value calculated.

> *e* This is certainly a possibility! You could carry out this method and do it in the way described. There is probably enough correct information here to award 2 of the maximum 4 marks.

(e) Many more people prefer to work from home and are able to do so because of the growth in computer technology and the Internet. It is no longer necessary in some jobs to come into an office every morning and work from there.

> *e* These are generally vague points that are being put forward, such as 'prefer to work' and 'no longer necessary', but there is the solid fact that this has been helped by the growth of technology. With 4 marks available, this answer would certainly be marked at the lower end of any scheme.

■ ■ ■

Answer to question 5: candidate B

(a) The largest numerical increases are to the north and west of the UK such as Wales, N. Ireland and Scotland. These could be described as peripheral regions within the UK and as such often receive the greatest amount of assistance from central government in order to attract industry. The south of England attracted the lowest percentage increases, although this was not always the lowest in numbers. The southeast and East Anglia, for example, had the lowest percentage increase but at 25,235 this was not the lowest in numbers. The lowest areas in numbers were in the east of England, East Midlands and Yorkshire & Humberside, and these were also in the lowest percentage category. The West Midlands and the northeast were somewhere in the middle of both categories. There seems to be a clear 'North/South divide' in terms of the percentage of new manufacturing jobs created by overseas investment.

> *e* This answer gives a clear view of the division between 'North' and 'South' and also indicates that the largest gains are peripheral. The candidate covers both numbers and relative importance and points out that percentages and numbers sometimes paint different pictures. Because of this it is possible to award this answer the maximum of 5 marks.

(b) The government, along with local authorities, can give financial incentives for firms to move into certain regions. Foreign companies are also attracted by a pleasant environment in which to build their factories along with the necessary sites being available at the right cost. Some regions have a better infrastructure than others and firms find this attractive along with the workforce that they want. Some regions have greater unemployment amongst women which could be attractive to a company; other firms may seek a skilled labour force.

e There are some good points in this answer but the overall impression is that it lacks the detail necessary for it to be credited at the highest level. An answer such as this would certainly benefit from details or examples being presented. Where the candidate has covered financial incentives, it would be much better if examples of these were included. Similarly with infrastructure, examples of roads, ports etc. would enhance an answer and certainly, with a limited amount of credit available, promote it to the highest level of marks.

(c) (i) The service sector is growing over the whole of the UK but there are certain areas where there has been concentrated growth. Southeast England has seen a large growth along with the southwest with its major tourist industry. East Anglia and certain towns in the south of England, such as Bournemouth, have seen growth as firms have relocated from London. Most major cities, such as Manchester, Birmingham and Edinburgh, have also seen growth in service employment.

e This is a comprehensive answer and would receive all the 3 marks available.

(ii) As manufacturing has declined, so the service sector has increased. In the 1980s and 1990s there was a large growth in the financial sector, such as insurance and banking, and this has led to huge service growth in southeast England. There has also been a growth in technology which again has produced a vast number of jobs, particularly connected with developments on the Internet.

e Some good points here, particularly where the growth in certain types of service is placed in a specific region. This answer would not reach the 4 mark maximum as it is too vague in other areas — 'growth in technology', for example.

(d) To show the numbers of people employed in the regions you could use the same map to show the regions but represent the information as a vertical bar. In Figure 1 there is simply a number printed on each region which does not give an immediate visual impact, but using a bar map would. Each of the ten figures needs to be translated into a bar whose length is proportional to the value it represents. In this case 1cm could represent 10,000 jobs. When drawing, it is important that the base of the bar is firmly located in the region it represents so that there can be no confusion in the mind of the reader. Each bar needs to be blocked in with the same colour.

e A good answer which selects a method, justifies that selection and then gives a reasonably comprehensive account of how to construct it. An alternative would have been to use a divided circle (pie chart) with ten segments.

(e) Modern technology offers the possibility that more employees can work from home with such technology as e-mail, fax and even video-conferencing. As long as people have a telephone link it is possible. Some telebanking services operate through a terminal at the worker's home.

> Good on the reasons why it is possible, but the candidate could have covered much more. The growth must also have occurred because it brings advantages to both the employee and the employer. Employees get a more flexible working time without the inconvenience of travelling to a specific workplace and it also suits working mothers, whose numbers have grown in the workforce in recent years. Employers are given access to a workforce that they could not employ but for these methods.

Social segregation

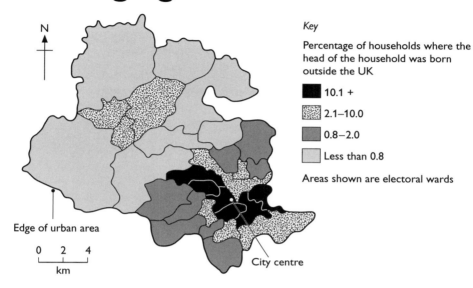

Key

Percentage of households where the head of the household was born outside the UK

■ 10.1 +

▨ 2.1–10.0

▨ 0.8–2.0

□ Less than 0.8

Areas shown are electoral wards

Edge of urban area

0 2 4
km

City centre

Figure 1 A city in England: distribution of immigrant population (1991 Census)

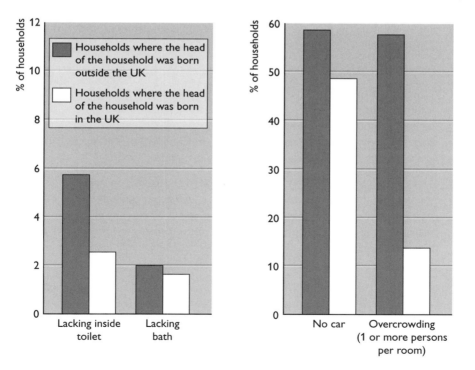

Figure 2 A city in England: measures of socio-economic well-being (1991 Census)

6

(a) Define the term 'social segregation'. (3 marks)

(b) (i) Describe the distribution of the immigrant population in the city shown in Figure 1. (4 marks)

(ii) Suggest reasons why such distributions occur in UK cities. (6 marks)

(c) In what ways does the immigrant population of the city shown in Figure 2 appear to have a poorer standard of living than the rest of the population? (5 marks)

(d) With reference to one or more named cities that you have studied, describe and suggest reasons for the social and demographic changes which have involved ethnic groups during the last 30 years. (7 marks)

Total: 25 marks

■ ■ ■

Answer to question 6: candidate A

(a) This is when people of different types live in different areas of the city from each other.

e This is defining the term at its most simple. The statement is certainly correct but needs some details on the definition of 'different' in this context, i.e. with some reference to ethnic or cultural origin, income or even age.

(b) (i) The immigrant population is mainly concentrated around the city centre with some towards the northern part of the city. There are few immigrants to the north and west.

e An answer that covers the obvious points and would receive moderate credit.

(ii) When migrants arrive in the UK they go to the cheapest housing which is often found towards the centre of the city. Once established in such places, they tend to stick together there for a number of reasons and, as a result, immigrant communities develop. Few immigrants are then willing to settle outside of these areas where their families and friends will be.

e There is enough material here for reasonable credit to be awarded, probably at the top of Level I in a mark scheme. What has been written is certainly true but lacks real detail which would take the credit into Level II. For example, 'a number of reasons' could have been explained. There is also a concentration on the map towards the edge of the urban area and the candidate could have made some reference to this.

(c) All the indicators show that the immigrants have a poorer standard of living. They have more people lacking an inside toilet and a bath. They have a greater number of houses with no car and they are also more overcrowded than those houses where people were born in the UK.

e The candidate has interpreted the data correctly but has seen the information only as a simple four-category exercise and the fact that the immigrant population is highest in each. This then gives them a poorer living standard. The candidate must do more to gain credit at the higher levels by, for example, describing the degree of difference, such as that shown with overcrowding, and by linking these indicators to low living standards.

(d) Ethnic groups have seen many changes over the last 30 years. They concentrated first of all in the poorest housing areas in the middle of cities such as Manchester, but have spread over time to other parts of the city and the surrounding towns, such as Bury, Bolton and Rochdale. At one time they kept very much to themselves but are now much more integrated into society with more mixed marriages and with mixed schooling. Their populations have risen as they tend to have a high birth rate. In Manchester, the Mosside area and that around Cheetham Hill are still regarded as the home of the immigrant community.

> *e* The candidate has identified some changes that have affected the ethnic community. For social change he/she has dealt with housing and integration, both of which are correct areas for this question, but it is also possible to deal with wealth, cultural development, religion, etc. References to one or more named cities is minimal — little more than 'such as Manchester'. Reference to the movement out to the surrounding towns is not strictly correct in terms of Greater Manchester, and the references to inner-city areas really needs more substance. This answer, therefore, can only be credited within Level I of a mark scheme.

■ ■ ■

Answer to question 6: candidate B

(a) Social segregation is the clustering together of people with similar characteristics into separate residential areas in a town or city. These characteristics may include ethnic and cultural origins, age group, income group or any other aspect of social class.

> *e* A comprehensive answer which would be awarded the maximum mark.

(b) (i) Immigrant groups in this city are mainly concentrated into two separate areas, the major one being around the city centre and the smaller one around wards towards the northwest of the city. The large concentration at the centre shows a linear grouping from east to northwest, but all wards shown in the highest category are close to the city centre. There are few immigrants in the outer regions to the north and west.

> *e* This is a comprehensive answer. Given the material on the map it would be difficult to write on any other aspect of the distribution of the immigrant population.

(ii) When most immigrants arrive in a new country they do not have a lot of money (that is probably why they are migrants in the first place) so they have to settle in the poorest parts of the city which contain the cheapest housing, i.e. the ones that they can afford. Once established, they will tend to stay, as

the services upon which they depend become established in the area. These are such things as community centres, their own language cinemas, clubs, shops serving their needs, etc. A strong sense of community grows up based upon culture, religion and language, and the concentration of migrants also acts as their security, all of which makes families reluctant to leave such areas. That is why the inner cities of the UK contain so many immigrant communities.

e A good answer which would certainly qualify for a mark within the highest levels of a mark scheme. The candidate, however, has concentrated exclusively on the inner-city areas and has not explained why patterns such as that in Figure 1 should grow up, where migrants have eventually begun to move into the suburbs.

(c) The immigrant population seems to have a poorer standard of living in all the indicators shown, although there are some significant differences between the measures. All the measures in Figure 2 are indicators of poverty and poor housing and the immigrant areas come worst off in each case. Twice as many immigrant houses lack an inside toilet than non-immigrant, although the difference in terms of having a bath is not as clear cut. Fewer migrants own a car, but the real difference comes when looking at the rate of overcrowding, as nearly 60% of immigrant homes are said to be overcrowded compared with about 15% of non-immigrants. From this evidence it is clear that immigrant communities are poorer than those that house the native population.

e An excellent answer that would certainly be awarded the maximum mark for this section. In fact, it is difficult to see what else the candidate could have written!

(d) Immigrants to a country often have a higher birth rate than the native population, although through time this tends to get less. Migrants once concentrated in the inner cities, but increasingly they have found themselves moving outwards to the suburbs. This has certainly been the case in major cities such as Manchester, Birmingham and Leeds. The ethnic population increasingly becomes integrated with the host population through mixed marriages and through work and social activities. Sometimes cultural strains develop within immigrant communities, particularly between the older, more traditional generations and the younger people. Links to 'homelands' are not always maintained, especially amongst the young, and the influence of religion, although strong, also declines.

e This is a good answer but it does lack the reference to 'one or more named cities that you have studied'. The candidate seems to have no idea of the situation in any city in the UK — all he/she can say is that one of the changes applies to Manchester, Birmingham and Leeds. Although this answer would be marked within Level II of a mark scheme, it would not be awarded the highest marks because of the lack of examples and because there is little reasoning behind the changes, which was requested in the wording of the question.